SILICON
LANDSCAPES

TITLES OF RELATED INTEREST

*Planning the urban region**
P. Self

The long wave in economic life
J. J. van Duijn

Why cities change
R. V. Cardew, J. V. Langdale & D. C. Rich (eds)

French planning in theory and practice
S. Estrin & P. Holmes

Collapse and survival: industry strategies in a changing world
R. Ballance & S. Sinclair

Planning in Europe
R. H. Williams (ed.)

The global textile industry
B. Toyne *et al.*

Blue gold: the political economy of natural gas
J. D. Davis

Future of the automobile†
A. A. Altshuler *et al.*

* Published in North America by the University of Alabama Press.
† Published in North America by MIT Press.

SILICON LANDSCAPES

Edited by

Peter Hall
University of Reading and University of California, Berkeley

Ann Markusen
University of California, Berkeley

Boston
ALLEN & UNWIN
London   Sydney

The book is largely derived from papers published in
Built Environment **9** (1).

Allen & Unwin Inc.,
Fifty Cross Street, Winchester, Mass 01890, USA

George Allen & Unwin (Publishers) Ltd,
40 Museum Street, London WC1A 1LU, UK

George Allen & Unwin (Publishers) Ltd,
Park Lane, Hemel Hempstead, Herts HP2 4TE, UK

George Allen & Unwin Australia Pty Ltd,
8 Napier Street, North Sydney, NSW 2060, Australia

First published in 1985

Library of Congress Cataloging in Publication Data

Main entry under title:
  Silicon landscapes.
Bibliography: p.
Includes index.
1. Microelectronics industry – California – Santa
Clara County.   2. Microelectronics industry –
England.   3. High technology industries –
California – Santa Clara County.   4. High
technology industries – England.   5. Industrial
districts – California – Santa Clara County.
6. Industrial districts – England.
I. Hall, Peter Geoffrey.   II. Markusen, Ann R.
HD9696.A3U5987 1984 338.4'76213817   84–20381
ISBN 0–04–338122–7 (alk. paper)
ISBN 0–04–338123–5 (pbk. : alk. paper)

British Library Cataloguing in Publication Data

  Silicon landscapes.
1. High technology industries
I. Hall, Peter, *1932–*   II. Markusen, Ann
338.4'7   HC79.H5
ISBN 0–04–338122–7
ISBN 0–04–38123–5 Pbk

Set in 10 on 12 point Palatino by Nene Phototypesetters Ltd
and printed in Great Britain by Mackays of Chatham

Preface

Silicon Valley, the legendary Californian land where the micro-processor was born, has produced a host of imitators: Silicon Prairie (the Dallas-Fort Worth area), Silicon Glen (Central Scotland), Software Valley (the Thames-Kennet Valley from Maidenhead to Newbury), and doubtless almost as many others as there are technological journalists. But it has produced not only names; it has brought forth a new economic Holy Grail, industrial renaissance through high-technology job creation. Every city in the advanced industrial world, it now seems, is struggling to open its science park as the answer to decaying steel mills and rusting automobile plants.

In all the enthusiasm, there is a singular lack of hard evidence. To a surprising extent, the necessary research has not yet been done. Some important work is now under way to try to establish just where, and why, high-technology industry has taken root – but this work has not yet produced reportable results. In the interim, we felt that it would be useful to establish just what is now known.

The logical places to start were the universities next door to the new developments. This book – an extended version of a special issue of the journal *Built Environment* – is effectively produced through the collaboration of academics at two research centres: the Institute of Urban and Regional Development at the University of California, Berkeley, on the other side of the San Francisco Bay from Silicon Valley; and the Joint Centre for Land Development Studies at the University of Reading/College of Estate Management, in the heart of the so-called M4 Corridor west of London. Both are engaged in research on the phenomenon of high-technology growth; this collection is the first place in which the results have been set out as a coherent whole.

The first chapter, by Peter Hall, is newly written for this book-length version. It analyses the fast-growing literature on long waves of economic development, and concludes that each of these waves (coming at approximately 55-year intervals since the first Industrial Revolution of the eighteenth century) has been marked by the rise of a new group of innovative industries – the high-technology group of their era – located in a new industrial region. The evidence suggests that we are now coming to the end of the fourth such long wave; the critical question is the nature of the coming fifth wave and its resulting geographical pattern.

The following group ot papers presents the American evidence and stems from work at the University of California, Berkeley. Chapter 2, by AnnaLee Saxenian, summarizes her work on the genesis and growth of Silicon Valley. It shows that to an extraordinary degree, Silicon Valley resulted from the drive and imagination of one man: Frederick Terman, Professor of Electrical Engineering at Stanford University. It was Terman who encouraged his graduates to set up infant businesses in the area close to the campus; who obtained major research contracts from the American government; who effectively set up the Stanford Research Institute and then created the world's first Science Park just outside the campus gates. The result, Saxenian reveals, was the creation of some 25,000 new jobs a year in the adjacent Santa Clara Valley during the 1970s.

The question is whether this miracle can be repeated. In Chapter 3, Ann Markusen is sceptical. She introduces material from a so-far unpublished major series of studies, commissioned by the then Governor of California Gerry Brown, on the prospects and job-creation capacities of high-technology industries in California. One such industry – studied by Markusen herself together with Barbara Wachsman, Richard Osborn and Peter Hall – focuses on the software industry, which has recently enjoyed a dizzying record of expansion in California. The research, summarized in Chapter 4, suggests that in the future this industry may not have a major potential for job creation; the necessary skills will be at the higher levels, while the production facilities may be automated or exported out of the area and even out of the state. Similarly, in another Californian glamour industry – biotechnology, reported in Chapter 5 by Marshall Feldman – there has been little job creation of any kind so far, because the industry barely exists. Marc Weiss, who coordinated these studies for Governor Brown, draws a controversial conclusion from them in Chapter 6: high technology will not be the panacea that many Americans expect, and consequently economic policy ought to put more emphasis on preserving the jobs that now exist.

This is a sobering introduction to the British contributions. Chapter 7, newly written for this collection by Ray Oakey of the Centre for Urban Development Studies at the University of Newcastle upon Tyne, provides a bridge between the two sets of studies by reporting on joint Anglo-American work on the role of small businesses in high-technology growth. He concludes that there are powerful agglomeration economies of a traditional kind which may lock new-entrant firms into a few select locations. In Chapter 8 Michael Breheny, Paul Cheshire and Robert Langridge report on their early investigations into the origins of Britain's nearest equivalent to the Silicon Valley phenomenon: the M4 Corridor from London to Bristol.

Their provisional conclusion is that local universities did not provide the initial stimulus; more probably, major government research establishments – especially in defence and in nuclear energy – did. And it is equally likely that much of the stimulus came from outside, in the form of American high-technology corporations – many from Silicon Valley itself – wanting to establish European beachheads close to London's Heathrow airport. Finally – echoing the American work – they conclude that even here, high technology has not been the cornucopia that many seek.

Continuing in this sceptical mood, in Chapter 9 Tony Taylor casts a dispassionate eye on the science park boom in Britain – and concludes that the term covers a multitude of different initiatives, many of them effectively old-fashioned industrial developments in new garb.

Finally, in Chapter 10 the editors discuss the implications of these findings for regional policy. In it we reveal a difference of view, which could be summed up as British pessimism versus American optimism. The pessimistic view is that the new high-technology industries tend to locate in regions and cities very different from those older industrial places which are now suffering the effects of de-industrialization – and that there is little that regional or urban policy can now do about this; because national economic priorities require the new industries to counter the decline of the old ones, we should encourage them wherever they choose to locate. The optimistic view is that by a positive use of national scientific and educational policy, we can steer the innovative industries into chosen older industrial locations – and that we should do this, because the social costs of failing to do so would be too great. Whatever our degree of pessimism or optimism, both of us are agreed on one important point: that selective regeneration of older industrial regions and cities is both feasible and highly desirable, and that the means to this end is by a new articulation of scientific-educational policies and regional-urban policies. That is the final word of this book, though doubtless not of the debate on its subject matter.

PETER HALL
ANN MARKUSEN
Berkeley/London, May 1984

Acknowledgements

Chapters 2–6 and 8–9 of this collection earlier appeared in *Built Environment*, Volume 9, Number 1, Spring 1983. Grateful thanks are due to Ann Drybrough-Smith of the Alexandrine Press, Oxford – publishers of *Built Environment* – for her numerous services in making this material available for publication in book form.

Chapter 1 is based in part on an article by the author which appeared in *Transaction/SOCIETY*, Volume 19, Number Five, July–August 1982.

Chapter 7 is based on work financed by a Designated Research Centre grant from the Economic and Social Research Council (ESRC) to the Centre for Urban and Regional Development Studies (CURDS) at the University of Newcastle upon Tyne.

Contents

List of contributors

Michael Breheny is Lecturer in the Department of Geography, University of Reading.

Paul Cheshire is Lecturer in the Department of Economics, University of Reading.

Marshall M. A. Feldman is Assistant Professor, College of Urban Affairs, Cleveland State University.

Peter Hall is Professor of Geography, University of Reading and University of California, Berkeley.

Robert Langridge is Research Officer in Economics and Geography at the University of Reading.

Ann R. Markusen is Associate Professor, Department of City and Regional Planning, University of California, Berkeley.

Ray Oakey is Research Associate, Centre for Urban and Regional Development Studies, University of Newcastle Upon Tyne.

Richard Osborn is a Research Assistant in the Institute of Urban and Regional Development, University of California, Berkeley.

AnnaLee Saxenian is Assistant Professor, Department of Urban Studies and Planning, Massachusetts Institute of Technology.

Tony Taylor is with the Centre for Advanced Land Use Studies, College of Estate Management.

Barbara Wachsman is a Research Assistant in the Institute of Urban and Regional Development, University of California, Berkeley.

Marc A. Weiss is Assistant Professor, School of Urban Planning and Policy, University of Illinois, Chicago.

1

The geography of the Fifth Kondratieff

PETER HALL

*If Kondratieff was right in his theory of the cyclical
nature of economic expansion and contraction – and history
has certainly lent some credence to that notion – what
are the lessons to be learned from the ending of the
fourth long wave, what will be the nature of the
fifth wave, and where will it take place?*

Geographers, economists, planners and politicians throughout the advanced industrial countries have recently been haunted by the spectre of deindustrialization. Whole regions and cities are suddenly gripped by a kind of economic plague: within a very short order, as their factories massively contract or close completely, their economic base crumbles and dies. This disease afflicts not merely regions traditionally vulnerable to the winds of economic fortune, like Central Scotland or South Wales and New England, but also areas formerly thought immune, like Britain's Birmingham and Coventry, America's New York City and Detroit.

The Anatomy of Job Loss

There has been one good result, in the form of a flood of academic literature – first and still foremost in Great Britain, now developing in the United States – which has thrown light on some of the causes. In particular, geographers – both in Great Britain and in the United States – have devoted sustained and productive research effort to what can be called, in a title from two of them, *The Anatomy of Job Loss* (Massey and Meegan, 1982). Working within a Political Economy tradition, these writers have shown how heavy employment losses in advanced industrial countries, during the recession of the late 1970s and early 1980s, represent a logical reaction of the system of capitalist production to increasing competition and falling profits.

At the bottom of it is a process that economists call the *product cycle*, and that some among them are starting to call the *profit cycle* (Markusen, 1984). In the earliest stages of development of an industrial product – be it cotton textiles, steel or cars – the necessary technical knowledge is limited to a few people in the most advanced industrial countries of the day. Later, the knowledge is progressively diffused to more and more people in more and more countries. These countries, which are at an earlier stage of economic development, often possess a very vigorous entrepreneur class. They are also apt to have large numbers of workers, pouring off the land and into the cities, happy to take work at almost any price. Details like trades unions, health and safety regulations, and pollution controls are often effectively absent. It is not surprising that plants in these countries can readily undercut the Americas and Great Britains of the world. This especially true because so many of these factories are now owned by mutinational corporations based on advanced industrial countries. As Ford and General Motors open plants in Mexico or Brazil, and the electronics companies open plants almost everywhere, the world increasingly becomes a single factory. A 'world car' may be literally that, with the engine coming from one country, the transmission from another, parts from several others. This is already a reality in Europe; it threatens soon to become the case in North America.

In these circumstances, the product cycle becomes a profit cycle: firms or plants in the advanced industrial countries, faced with competition from the newly industrializing countries, can react only by cutting costs – which means shedding expensive labour. Massey and Meegan demonstrate that in Great Britain job losses have arisen from three causes: *greater productivity* through the introduction of new and more efficient processes; *failure to compete* resulting in closure; and *rationalization* where a multiplant enterprise shuts down certain factories in order to concentrate production on others (Massey and Meegan, 1982). Harrison's work on the New England economy has shown that such processes lead to a shedding of labour that does not, so far, manage to find alternative jobs demanding equivalent skills, and so is displaced into low-skill service-occupation employments (Bluestone and Harrison, 1982; Harrison, 1982).

The obsession with deindustrialization has brought forth an appropriate antidote, which for a time became almost an American political buzz word: *reindustrialization*. It is easy to see why industrialists, politicians and economists should all, in their mutual anxiety, grasp at such a miracle cure. They should however try to recall their classical education, if any: *re* is a Latin root meaning backwards. Reindustrialization, taken too literally, is a recipe for trying to re-create the glories of a lost industrial past – which, like any other exercise in nostalgia, is a fatal guide to industrial policy. Britain has gone down this road for a long time, by subsidizing uneconomic coal mines and steel mills; it is no accident that in the process, the British economy became the sickest in Europe.

The fact is that economic history, like any other kind of history, never quite repeats itself. Industries and regions, once on the way down, are apt not to come up. And if they ever do, they make it not by rediscovering past economic traditions, but by inventing new ones. New England textile towns lost out to competition from the South, but then made a partial comeback in electronics. Western mining towns became ghost towns and then flourishing tourist resorts. Reading in England was a sleepy biscuit- and beer-making town until it was invaded by decentralized offices from London and high-technology factories from California (see Chapter 8).

The Anatomy of Job Creation

In comparison with our knowledge of job contraction, we do not understand – a few limited exceptions apart – the parallel process of job creation. Even in the most severe depression since the 1930s, it is clear that certain regions and certain industries are growing. The contraction of employment in older industrial staples like textiles, deep coal mining, steel manufacture and shipbuilding is parallelled by an expansion of such newer industries as electronics and aerospace, as well as producer services such as finance, insurance and real estate. But, though to some extent these processes can be traced everywhere, clearly they result in pronounced regional shifts: the new industries tend to grow in places different from those where the old industries are contracting. Central Scotland, the English North East and Merseyside, the Middle Atlantic and East North Central regions, are the contracting economies; East Anglia and the South West region of England, and the American Sunbelt, are the complementary areas of growth.

It seems time, then, to shift focus. Are there parallel forces in contemporary capitalism that lead to the birth and growth of new industrial traditions, just as others lead to decay and death of older ones? The limited recent work gives some clues. In particular, the meticulous work of David Birch on the American economy (Birch, 1979) suggests that the important processes in both expansion and decline consist in the birth rates of new firms and the death rates of both new and old ones. Many firms are born, in every region; but many soon die. However, of those that survive, a few show rapid growth and hence contribute powerfully to total job gain. In older industrial regions like the Northeast, there are fewer firm births to compensate for the high death rate; so there are fewer firms available to expand. In newer regions, for reasons not entirely clear, there are more births of new firms. In Great Britain, some work on older inner cities (Dennis, 1978; Lloyd and Mason, 1978; Dicken and Lloyd, 1978) suggests a similar dominance of birth and death processes; the main reason why these areas are contracting is that many firms die while relatively few are born. In both countries, actual movement of firms or plants is a far less important factor in explaining the overall pattern of regional economic growth.

Here, some episodes from economic history may provide a useful clue. In Britain in the 1890s, both Glasgow and Birmingham prospered – Glasgow on the basis of its great shipbuilding and marine engineering yards, Birmingham on the basis of small workshops that made a bewildering variety of small tools, guns and bicycles. Thence, Glasgow stuck to building ships – even after 1950, when new competitors entered the market and world demand failed to keep pace. But Birmingham constantly adapted: as the market for bicycles became satiated, it switched to cars. In the thirty years after World War Two, Glasgow declined while Birmingham boomed. The Glasgow economic historian Sidney Checkland, pondering the reasons for Glasgow's failure, borrowed a metaphor from Robert Louis Stevenson: the Upas tree of the South Pacific, whose foliage spread so wide as to kill any vegetation in its shade (Checkland, 1975). In the same way, the energies of Glaswegians were so absorbed in building ships that they caused any other enterprise to wither. Checkland shows that in the 1920s Glasgow had infant truck and automobile industries but they died or moved away. Birmingham, but still more London and its surrounding area, stood in sharp contrast. In the 1930s – a period that most Britons still regard as the darkest ever in economic terms – the economies of these areas showed remarkable growth. Whole new industries were created, lining the arterial highways of London's suburbs: processed foods, pharmaceuticals, vehicles, electrical goods, and many others. The 1930s, contrary to popular views, represented one of the more buoyant periods in British economic history.

Three Success Stories

More recently, the postwar success stories of three nations, two of them defeated in war – West Germany, France and Japan – illustrate the same point. In 1945, much of Germany's industrial past was buried in rubble. But in the 1950s came the economic miracle, its essence consisting in the Germans' ability to provide the consumer goods that people wanted. One of the most important was an absurdly shaped car, designed in 1934 by the distinguished automobile engineer Ferdinand Porsche for Adolf Hitler as the People's Car. When British car manufacturers toured Germany after World War Two, they were offered the Volkswagen factory; they turned the offer down, saying the car had no future.

Even more recently, the French economy has shown a spectacular rate of growth. Aided by a strong alliance between government and private industry, the French have gambled audaciously on a plan to become one of the most technologically advanced countries in the world. Sometimes this leads to costly blunders like the Concorde airplane, which the French shared with the British. But it also leads to the spectacular new rapid transit system in Paris, the even more advanced one recently completed in Lille, the new high-speed rail link now open between Paris and Lyon, and the plan to give a computer terminal to every French telephone subscriber. The aim of these plans is not just to modernize France; it is to make the country a living showplace of technology, to serve as a base for export orders. And it seems to be working.

But the most spectacular example of such a policy – and, indeed, a model for the French – is Japan. The most significant aspect of the Japanese story is, however, apt to be neglected in some bastions of free enterprise like the contemporary United States and Great Britain: it is the systematic and ruthless partnership between the government, in the form of the Ministry of International Trade and Industry (MITI), and private industry. MITI, in the last quarter century, has systematically sought to identify the large new industrial markets of the future – and has then exploited them, by pouring state money into the crucial initial stage of research and development. Then, at a certain point, it has made its exit, having carefully arranged for one or more companies to take over mass production. It did exactly this with colour television in the early 1970s, to such an extent that Japanese sets overran the American and European markets. In 1983, it is doing the same with home computers.

The moral of all this is clear: economic success lies with the country and the region and the city that innovate, that keep one step ahead of the action. Such innovation has two key elements, both of which must be present for the trick to happen. There must first be some breakthrough, generally but not necessarily technical in character. (It can also be in organization and marketing. Ray Kroc did not invent the hamburger, but he did invent a new way of organizing hamburger sales when he purchased the modest San Bernardino business of the McDonald brothers. Similarly, Kemmens Wilson did not invent the hotel, but when he opened the first Holiday Inn in Memphis, Tennessee, he did pioneer a new concept of standardized hotels of uniform quality, with instant nationwide room reservations.) There must always be the ability to recognize what will sell; in the celebrated aphorism of the great American entrepreneur Henry Kaiser, to find a need and fill it.

Innovations and Long Waves

This dual nature of technical innovation is important. It means that technical developments *per se* are not of much significance. They may never become innovations, in the sense of becoming commercially useful; or they may do so only after years or decades of further development. Technical developments without commercial viability include some of the great commercial disasters of economic history, like the aforementioned Concorde airplane. Conversely, relatively simple developments can prove spectacular successes if they meet a need. It was no spectacular scientific breakthrough when – in Atlanta, Georgia in 1886 – a local drug merchant mixed together some ingredients in a formula for a new soft drink. But the customers liked it, not merely in Atlanta but eventually across most of the world.

The dual character of innovation is not a new idea. It was a key concept in a classic of economic analysis: Joseph Schumpeter's *Business Cycles*, written in the late 1930s (Schumpeter, 1939, 1982). His thesis was that every so often in economic history, several innovations in the true sense – that is, commercially utilizable inventions – bunched together to produce a rapid economic expansion. Thus for Schumpeter the so-called Industrial Revolution was just the first in a series. Based on developments in cotton spinning and weaving and in the smelting and refining of iron, plus the steam engine, it occurred from approximately 1785 to 1842. Then there was a second revolution, based on railroads and the Bessemer process in steel; it ran from 1842 to about 1895. The third industrial revolution was based on the chemical industry and on the beginnings of the electrical and auto industries; it started in the mid-1890s and had almost run its course when Schumpeter was writing in the 1930s.

In developing his thesis, Schumpeter leaned fairly heavily on an obscure paper, written in the early 1920s by a Moscow professor who later died in one of Stalin's jails. Nikolai Kondratieff was director of a Moscow research institute, and his paper – published in Russian in 1924 – had been translated and published in Germany in 1926, in a journal Schumpeter had helped to edit before emigrating to the United States. Only in 1935 was it published in the United States

(Kondratieff, 1935). Following a Marxist line of analysis, Kondratieff argued that capitalist development followed a regular cycle, of about fifty-five years, from boom to bust and then to boom again. The triggering mechanism – so Kondratieff argued in a mere sentence – was technological development, which created new economic opportunities and thus generated economic expansion. But, after a time, these industries found their markets saturated, and so recession and then depression ensued, until a new wave of innovation set the whole process off again.

Schumpeter refined this theory, arguing that two shorter cycles were laid over the long Kondratieff waves – the Juglar, eight to ten years long, corresponding to the classic 'trade cycle', and the Kitchen, a short cycle only just over three years long. The complex interrelationship between these cycles, he hypothesized, should explain the process of economic expansion and contraction in modern capitalism – the process of creative destruction, as he termed it. Attempting to prove it, he traced the course of economic history since the first Industrial Revolution in meticulous detail, almost month by month. The result seemed positive, though Schumpeter – no believer in precise mathematical modelling, despite his own considerable competence in the field – never subjected it to rigorous analysis.

Economists are disputatious folk. It was small wonder that as soon as such a prestigious professor had embraced the Kondratieff notion, another should try to demolish it. Already, in his 1940 review of Schumpeter's book, Simon Kuznets doubted the validity of the long wave theory (Kuznets, 1940). In his subsequent life's work, which gained him the Nobel prize in economics, Kuznets did what Schumpeter had eschewed: to gather a mass of data and to model it, so as to establish economic history on a quantitative basis (Kuznets, 1930, 1946, 1966). At the end of some thirty years of work, he concluded that the time series of national income – derived from several advanced industrial countries – provided no evidence for the Kondratieff thesis. Instead, he claimed, they strongly suggested a twenty-year cycle of expansion and contraction.

There the matter might have rested, but for a nagging point about the Kondratieff–Schumpeter theory. It should have predicted a bad slump around 1930, an economic revival in the 1930s (when Schumpeter was writing), a boom in the 1950s and early 1960s, and a descent into depression in the 1970s. It is small wonder that in the 1980s, a number of people are again taking Kondratieff–Schumpeter very seriously. These include the flourishing school of political economists working within the Marxist tradition, for whom the thesis is particularly appealing. The Belgian Marxist Ernest Mandel, for instance, makes the long waves a principal feature of his major tome on *Late*

Capitalism, and has subsequently written a shorter book particularly on the subject (Mandel, 1975, 1980). Other economists, working within different traditions – such as W. W. Rostow, originator of the celebrated theory of Stages of Economic Growth – have also embraced the notion (Rostow, 1978). The global modeller Jay Forrester has suggested that Kuznets's cycles may nest inside Kondratieff ones (Forrester, 1976; see also Forrester, 1981).

A major additional reason why the long waves are again receiving attention is a remarkable book by a German scholar. Published originally in 1974, but not translated into English until 1979, Gerhard Mensch's *Technological Stalemate: Innovations overcome the Depression* is a breathtakingly original and stimulating attempt to provide detailed substantiation of the original Kondratieff thesis. Mensch assembles data for hundreds of technical innovations – that is, inventions that actually came to be applied in industry – from the first Industrial Revolution onwards. He traces in detail the progress from original technical breakthrough to industrial innovation, and emerges with what seems to be a remarkable finding. This is that in some periods the process of application is very slow, while in others it speeds up. The result is what Mensch calls a waggon-train effect, whereby many innovations occur almost simultaneously within a few years. The peak years for such clustering – what Mensch calls radical years of history – were 1764, 1825, 1886 and 1935. These, he argues, almost exactly correspond to the dates of the long waves originally identified by Kondratieff and described by Schumpeter.

But Mensch does not stop there. Because the process is a very regular one, he is able to go on and predict it. He does this not by any simple extrapolation from past data, but by a complex technique that involves looking at the actual pace of innovation in the recent past. According to this analysis, by the mid-1970s fully half of all the innovations for the next Kondratieff upswing had already reached the stage of commercial applicability. The next radical year of history, Mensch announces with a flourish, will be 1989. And the decade of maximum innovation will start in that most symbolic of years, 1984. If the theory holds good, however, the boom will come long after 1984. Past experience indicates that generally an economic upswing will happen between eleven and seventeen years after the peak of innovation. On that basis, the effect on the world economy will not be felt until well into the 1990s. The picture would be one of world depression throughout the 1980s – a daunting prospect.

Recently, Mensch's thesis has been beginning to get a great deal of attention – meaning a great deal of criticism. In summer 1981 the journal of prediction, *Futures*, devoted a whole issue to the subject of long waves, including an attack on the Mensch thesis by members of

the Science Policy Research Unit at the University of Sussex, England
(Clark, Freeman and Soete, 1981). They claimed that much of the data
he used were vaguely dated and that he had left out important
innovations that might weaken his argument. Also, following Kuznets and using the available data on economic growth, they could not
systematically trace a 55-year wave. In subsequent work the same
team have accepted the existence of Kondratieff long waves but have
continued to dispute the Mensch hypothesis that innovation bun-
ching is the explanation (Freeman, Clark and Soete, 1982). They
incline rather to a thesis that is shared by Marxist writers like Mandel:
that the waves are triggered by exogenous forces of an almost
accidental nature. Thus both the Sussex team and Mandel believe that
the long wave starting around the time of World War Two was partly
triggered by the rearmament boom of the 1930s, by the war itself and
by the subsequent Cold War.

Meanwhile another most important contribution to the debate has
appeared, again in translation, from the Dutch economist van Duijn
(van Duijn, 1983). Apart from showing that the theory had been
developed by other economists before Kondratieff – notably by the
pre-World War One Dutch writer van Gelderen – van Duijn makes a
major discovery: that the long waves appear much more clearly from
the data if they are assumed to be superimposed on another, even
deeper, wave representing the Rostowian curve of economic growth.
In the mid-1980s, then, there is a great deal of agreement that the long
waves – as well as other, shorter economic perturbations – exist; what
is still at issue is their cause, and in particular the question of whether
they are generated by some kind of automatic, internal regulating
machinery inside the capitalist economic system itself. If that proved
true, of course, it would mean that Kondratieff had made a major
nonsense of Marx's central thesis of deepening capitalist crisis – which
is one good reason, perhaps, why Stalin should have locked him up,
and why the latter-day Marxist economists are so concerned to
disprove the notion.

The Geography of Innovation

What is significant is that all workers in the field do seem agreed that
long cycles exist; they disagree only on their length and on the
explanation of their occurrence. From this, it seems logical to conclude
that different long waves can and do occur in different countries and
even in different regions. Accepting for a moment the Kondratieff–
Schumpeter framework, then clearly the first and second waves were
dominated by Great Britain, though the United States and Germany

began to emerge during the second; the third was dominated by these two countries; in the fourth, which can be dated from World War Two until approximately the present time, the United States was predominant with Japan just beginning to appear on the stage. Further, within Great Britain the first wave was dominated by Lancashire, Shropshire and the Black Country; the second by newer regions like South Wales and the North East; the third and fourth by the West Midlands and Greater London.

New industrial traditions, in other words, took root in places different from older ones. Traditional explanations, like available raw materials, might be a factor here – especially in the earlier, more material-dependent, stages of economic growth. But they could not provide the only or even the main explanation why, for instance, the fledgling automobile industry should set itself up in Coventry and in Detroit rather than in (for instance) Glasgow or Baltimore. The evolution of older and closely related industrial traditions (such as bicycles in Coventry) provides one explanation; so does the accidental presence of key industrialists. But perhaps one necessary condition was the very lack of very old-established industrial traditions, such as shipbuilding in Glasgow, which inhibited the growth of new and delicate industrial vegetation: the Upas Tree effect (Checkland, 1975).

Lack of such an inhibiting inheritance, then, can be regarded as a necessary condition for the development of new industrial traditions – but surely not a sufficient one. In the American Sunbelt, for instance, there are many possible areas where new industries might have taken root, but in only a few did this actually happen. The map of the 1980 United States Census, for instance, shows that many Sunbelt areas, especially in the 'Old South', experienced population loss in the 1970s (Hauser, 1981, p. 54). Thus there has to be some other factor or factors. Studies among industrialists indicate that 'favourable business climate' is a factor quoted by many establishing branch operations in the Sunbelt (Weinstein and Firestine, 1978); yet even this cannot explain the spatial variations that occur. Since the sources of Sunbelt economic growth are varied – ranging from high-technology industry to recreation and retirement – one should expect that the precise triggering mechanisms will similarly vary.

One plausible hypothesis is that growth of a relatively small industrial base – especially in innovative, high-technology industry and associated producer services – can create a very large income and employment multiplier effect in the form of construction, real estate, recreation and personal service industries. Much of this multiplier effect will be felt in the immediate local economy, but some will occur at greater distances, especially in accessible recreation areas. Thus the growth of ski resorts in the Colorado Rockies or the California Sierra can be ascribed in part to demand generated in the metropolitan areas of Denver-Boulder or San Francisco-Oakland, one hundred and more miles away.

No geographer, as yet, appears to have teased out these connections – important as they are for understanding the contemporary geography of growth. But central to the whole process is the triggering of the new basic industry, which provides the rationale for it. We know from limited studies of the subject that high-technology industry seems to stem from basic R&D either in universities or in specialized research laboratories, both public and private. Malecki's work on American R&D shows it to be fairly well-distributed across the United States, both Frostbelt and Sunbelt, with strong concentrations in larger metropolitan areas (Malecki, 1980a, 1980b, 1981a, 1981b). However, what is more difficult to identify is the distribution of the basic R&D that contributes to new industrial development: what in the jargon are called product innovations as distinct from process innovations. Recent research suggests strongly that these product innovations are sharply bunched in time and that major periods of job creation follow them; in contrast, succeeding periods of process innovation lead first to stagnation, then to contraction of employment (Rothwell, 1982). The unconfirmed suspicion is that product innovations are quite highly concentrated in certain places.

The classic case is of course Silicon Valley. Located between San Jose and Palo Alto in the San Francisco Bay Area, the Santa Clara Valley is the centre of microprocessor and associated industries in the United States. Since 1950 it has been the fastest growing industrial area in the United States; during the last decade it has added, on average, 25,000 new jobs a year. It sits next door to Stanford University, and that is no accident; as shown by AnnaLee Saxenian (see Chapter 2), it was the brainchild of Frederick Terman, a Stanford professor (see also Saxenian, 1981). In the 1920s, Terman started to encourage his electrical engineering graduates to stay in the area and set up small business there. Two of the first, William Hewlett and David Packard, started theirs in a garage near the campus in 1939; it is now one of the largest electronics firms in the world. But most of the firms were set up in the 1950s and 1960s – by which time Terman, by then a senior figure at Stanford, had persuaded his university to build a special industrial park to house them. Thus, by a deliberate set of policies, was Silicon Valley born.

Similarly, the concentration of the new biotechnology complex of industries in the San Francisco Bay Area seems to stem directly from basic university R&D – through such individuals as Professor Herbert Boyer of the University of California San Francisco Medical Faculty, who is a founder–director of Genentech, the San Francisco-based genetic engineering firm. Genentech stock rose from $35 to $80 within one minute of being placed on the stock market in October 1980. It subsequently sunk to a less euphoric level – which was understandable, since it had no record of earnings at all, and since there was no other company in the world with which it could be compared. The fever has even gripped major public institutions. In summer 1981, various branches of the University of California were discovered in an unseemly scramble to start a genetic engineering venture, together with a private developer, on Alameda island in the San Francisco Bay. The bid failed, but they have vowed to go back into the business. They cannot afford not to exploit the potential gains from their own research – or so they say. Much of the critical work so far has been done on Boyer's San Francisco campus.

In England, the scanty available evidence indicates that – with the possible exception of the Cambridge area, where a whole host of small firms seems to have spun off from university research – the presence of a major university has not been a major factor in the development of new high-technology industry. In the outstanding British example of the growth of such industry – the so-called M4 Corridor west of London (Anon, 1982; Feder, 1983; Neil, 1983; Thomas, 1983; Walker, 1983) – the key factor seems to have been the dense concentration of government scientific establishments in the Reading–Newbury–Oxford triangle. Previous research indicates that the British South East region, within which the heart of the M4 Corridor lies, has both the highest concentration of R&D (Buswell and Lewis, 1970; Howells, 1984) and a high proportion of innovative firms (Oakey, Thwaites and Nash, 1980).

Of these two possible sources of R&D, universities and research laboratories, it seems clear that both had origins that were often fairly arbitrary. Stanford University was the result of a gift by the railroad entrepreneur Leland Stanford in the late nineteenth century, and is established on land donated when the area was almost completely rural. Government research laboratories, in both Britain and the United States, seem often to have been located for strategic reasons – in particular, relative freedom from air attack – in World War Two. (Certainly this was a crucial factor in the establishment of the Lawrence Berkeley and Lawrence Livermore Laboratories in California.) Very often there seems to have been no pressing location factor; there were no original advantages of intellectual agglomeration, though these may have been produced internally as a result of the expansion of the facility concerned.

Innovation and the Agglomeration Effect

The precise point is that once the critical decision had been taken, these institutions became a force for further development, creating intellectual 'external economies' for new firms setting up close to them and even directly depending on subcontracts from them. Once the process was under way, then – as has been documented both for Silicon Valley and for the Highway 128 development around Boston, Massachusetts – a process of regular spin-off occurred, whereby new firms would be created by entrepreneurs splitting away from a parent firm. However, since all the firms depended on the same skilled labour pool and access to scarce information, they tended to remain tied in close proximity to each other: a new, high-technology version of the traditional industrial quarter first described in a classic passage by Alfred Marshall:

> When an industry has chosen a locality for itself, it is likely to stay there long: so great are the advantages which people following the same skilled trade get from near neighbourhood to one another. The mysteries of the trade become no mysteries; but are as it were in the air, and children learn many of them unconsciously. Good work is rightly appreciated, inventions and improvements in machinery, in processes and the general organization of the business have their merits promptly discussed: if one man starts a new idea, it is taken up by others and combined with suggestions of their own; and thus it becomes the source of further new ideas. And presently subsidiary trades grow up in the neighbourhood, supplying it with implements and materials, organizing its traffic, and in many ways conducing to the economy of its material (Marshall, 1920, p. 225).

That was true of the traditional industrial quarter in the inner areas of the great Victorian cities, such as the clothing and furniture quarters of East London (Hall, 1962; Martin, 1966) and the jewellery and gun quarters of Birmingham (Wise, 1951); it is equally true of a high-technology area like Silicon Valley. What has changed is the original propulsive influence and hence the location. For the Victorian quarters it was the merchant houses, which were traditionally associated with the fringe of the central business district; for Silicon Valley it is venture capital which may be found on a regional or even a national scale, coupled with the knowledge of R&D that stems from the university and more widely from the scientific infrastructure of the area. So the industrial quarter is no longer locked in to the inner city; in contrast, it tends to look for high-amenity areas capable of attracting a highly-qualified, highly-paid, highly-mobile workforce (Berry,

1970). In the jargon of the economists, such places offer psychic income. And, to attract already highly-paid and scarce scientists and technicians, that is an important factor.

Indeed, it could be vital. These new industries do not locate near coal or iron or port facilities, or any of the 'factors of location' that traditionally decorated geography textbooks. Their material inputs, as in the case of silicon chips, may indeed be almost weightless. What is critical is, first, the general atmosphere of scientific excitement and advance; second, an agreeable environment in both a physical and a social sense; and third – arising out of the other two – what the economists call the external economies of agglomeration, which create a powerful inertia effect. For computer scientists, leaving Silicon Valley would be like getting off the world. In the Valley, everyone talks and breathes computers. They even have their local trade newspaper, the *Silicon Valley Gulch*. Cut off from this, like a fish out of water, their creative energies may just die.

Innovation and the Older Cities

This has profound implications. For it means that the new industry is likely to be found in regions and in areas quite different from the old. Indeed, the image of the old industrial city – committed to dying industries produced by traditional methods with an ageing workforce resistant to change, with a depressing physical environment that is unattractive to mobile workers, and perhaps lacking the necessary research expertise in the new technologies – is just about as repellent to the new industries as could be imagined. The new industry, then, will seek positively to avoid such places. This may help explain why, despite a history of vigorous intervention in regional policies since World War Two, the British have been so unsuccessful in attracting new industry into the older cities. Insofar as the policy had some success, it was to attract a range of such new industry into the suburban, exurban and new town areas beyond commuting range of these cities. Thus, ironically, it had the effect of hastening the outflow of population from these cities, which by the late 1960s and 1970s had reached American proportions.

We can logically ask whether, in such circumstances, the inner cities in the older industrial regions have any economic future at all. They have an ageing and often outworn infrastructure, which is reaching an age when it demands complete renewal. They have increasingly a residual labour force composed of those who could not or would not join the exodus, and which contains disproportionate numbers of the hard-to-employ. They have a depressing physical environment and

often suffer from poor transportation linkages compared with suburban and exurban areas. And they suffer from a lack of innovative
entrepreneurship: the Upas Tree effect. They lack the right milieu
(Hall, 1981).

They have, in other words, little going for them. Determined
policies, accompanied by liberal front-end government money, may
succeed in creating some kinds of work there: low-paid assembly
industry of the Third World type; similarly low-paid work in service
industries associated with recreational or tourist developments (conference and exhibition centres, theme parks); some regional-scale
office developments, mainly involved in routine data processing (and
subject to technological change that may displace some labour and
create a demand for special skills which such areas lack). Some such
developments, at least, would appear to match demands for certain
kinds of labour with the supply of them. None of them however
promises to develop truly entrepreneurial industrial traditions, such
as were once nourished in the inner city. That role has passed to the
outer city.

The only exception could occur if an R&D tradition, either already
existing in the inner city or deliberately implanted in it, could be used
on the Silicon Valley model to create a new entrepreneurial tradition.
In 1935, after all, the Santa Clara Valley had no high-technology
tradition at all; it was a fruit-growing area. Similarly, the Research
Triangle of North Carolina, deliberately located between the University of North Carolina and Duke University, has transformed the
research map of eastern North America. And in the United States there
are universities, like the University of Texas and the University of
Colorado, that are edging into the top league and that may spawn new
industrial complexes.

The problem is that the University of Texas campus at Austin, and
the University of Colorado campus at Boulder, share with Research
Triangle and Silicon Valley an exceptionally pleasant environment.
Still unproven is whether the same trick can be performed in the very
different and less prepossessing environment of the older industrial
city. Such an attempt is being made in Pittsburgh, where Carnegie-
Mellon University – an old-established university with a strong
technological tradition – is developing an experiment in computer
literacy for every student, sufficient to guarantee that all graduates will
emerge as sophisticated in computer applications. The hope is that in
turn they will set up new infant industries within the Pittsburgh area,
so giving it an alternative industrial structure to replace the contracting steel and heavy engineering base. Located some three miles from
Pittsburgh's Golden Triangle, Carnegie-Mellon can fairly be regarded
as an inner-city university. A similar thrust in the direction of

high-technology, campus-linked industry is evident at the University of Salford in England, an inner-city campus located in an area of industrial decline in the Greater Manchester conurbation.

Such bold strategies may succeed, but they are likely to take a long time to produce substantial results. At Stanford, as already seen, Terman started his activities in the 1930s; but it was not until the 1950s and 1960s that substantial numbers of new jobs began to be created. On this analogy, an inner-city high-technology strategy might be expected, if successful, to show real results around the turn of the century. And it must be stressed that in the interim, high existing levels of unemployment will almost certainly demand alternative, complementary measures to deal with them. The conclusion is that no single strategy, but rather a combination of different approaches, will be appropriate.

However, even then there is a limitation. Not every declining industrial city has a major university with a strong technological emphasis. It is highly likely indeed that in any advanced industrial economy there will only be room for a strictly limited number of such high-techology industries. To attempt to develop such concentrations all over the country may be self-contradictory and fruitless – particularly as the Silicon Valleys and Research Triangles have a head start.

An R&D Based Regional Strategy

The question naturally arises as to the main emphasis of such R&D strategies. That may be expected to differ from place to place, but to draw as far as feasible on adaptation of older industrial traditions. Three major likely areas for future industrial growth have been identified in a number of publications. First, the whole complex of computer applications, information systems and automatic control systems (robotics). These may increasingly differentiate themselves as separate industries, since they are likely to constitute the main economic base in advanced industrial countries. Secondly, the biotechnological group of industries, including agricultural and medical applications. And thirdly, the development of alternative sources of energy coupled with energy conservation devices. It is highly likely that these streams may merge and interrelate, as for instance in the development of computer systems for energy exploration or energy conservation, or the application of biotechnological research to the problem of generating artificial intelligence.

Policies for developing such new industries may range from the highly decentralized and dispersed to the highly centralized and coordinated. In almost all industralized countries, however, there is some degree of national coordination of R&D efforts. Governments consciously try to cooperate with the private sector in the development of new areas, whether for military reasons (a powerful force in the early development of Silicon Valley) or for reasons of economic development. These governmental efforts, by definition, will have spatial impacts. The question is whether governments could or should pursue a conscious strategy of urban and regional development based on R&D policies.

To do so, as already suggested, will in many cases mean swimming against the economic tide; the question is whether such policies could be successful. The British government, for instance, wanted to base its subsidized private manufacture of memory chips, through the British subsidiary of the American firm INMOS, in an Assisted Area – that is, one of the older and more problematic industrial regions. The returning expatriate members of the company resisted this move and instead located their headquarters in Bristol, an environmentally-attractive city with a good reputation in high-technology industry; later, under government pressure, they agreed to locate the manufacturing capacity across the Severn estuary in South Wales.

This however is perhaps an unfortunate example, since the entrepreneurs concerned were by no means new entrants. The right strategy might well be the Stanford or Carnegie-Mellon one: to bias government R&D spending to favour certain inner-city universities in the Assisted Areas. Such a policy, however, would tend to run up against the tradition in most western countries of relative autonomy in the granting of university research funds. In Great Britain the Science and Engineering Research Council, or in the United States the National Science Foundation, all dispose of funds without direct government interference on the principle of supporting the best centres. If government were to intervene it might well provoke loud protest from the scientific establishment and the charge that money was going to second-rate institutions.

There does not seem to be any easy reconciliation of these arguments. The best may sometimes be the enemy of the good. But perhaps there is a way out: in most countries, there are some inner-city centres of excellence in some fields. These should be differentially encouraged through government R&D funding (perhaps through the establishment of regional quotas to the research councils) and this scheme should be coupled with another, to provide venture capital to graduates of these universities to set up new local enterprises. In such a way, without undue violence to scientific susceptibilities, new industrial traditions may be implanted to replace the old.

References

Anon (1982) Britain's Sunrise Strip. *The Economist*, 30 January.

Berry, B. J. L. (1970) The geography of the United States in the year 2000, *Institute of British Geographers. Transactions*, **51**, pp. 21–53.

Birch, D. L. (1979) *The Job Generation Process* (MIT Program on Neighbourhood and Regional Change). Cambridge, Mass: Massachusetts Institute of Technology.

Bluestone, B. and Harrison, B. (1982) *The Deindustrialization of America: Plant Closings, Community Abandonment, and the Dismantling of Basic Industry*. New York: Basic Books.

Buswell, R. J. and Lewis, E. W. (1970) The geographical distribution of industrial research activity in the United Kingdom. *Regional Studies*, **4**, pp. 297–306.

Checkland, S. (1975) *The Upas Tree*. Glasgow: Glasgow University Press.

Clark, J., Freeman, C. and Soete, L. (1981) Long waves, inventions and innovations. *Futures*, **13**, pp. 308–22.

Dennis, R. (1978) The decline of manufacturing employment in Greater London. *Urban Studies*, **15**, pp. 63–73.

Dicken, P. and Lloyd, P. E. (1978) Inner metropolitan industrial change. Enterprise structures and policy issues: case studies of Manchester and Merseyside. *Regional Studies*, **12**, pp. 181–97.

Feder, B. J. (1983) Britain's Science Corridor. *New York Times*, 24 April.

Forrester, J. (1976) Business structure, economic cycles, and national policy. *Futures*, **8**, pp. 195–214.

Forrester, J. (1981) Innovation and economic change. *Futures*, **13**, pp. 323–31.

Freeman, C., Clark, J. and Soete, L. (1982) *Unemployment and Technical Innovation*. London: Frances Pinter.

Hall, P. G. (1962) *The Industries of London since 1861*. London: Hutchinson University Library.

Hall, P. (ed.) (1981) *The Inner City in Context: The Final Report of the Social Science Research Council Inner Cities Working Party*. London: Heinemann Education.

Harrison, B. (1982) *Rationalization, Restructuring, and Industrial Reorganization in Older Regions: The Economic Transformation of New England since World War II*. Cambridge, Mass: Joint Center for Urban Studies of the Massachusetts Institute of Technology and Harvard University.

Hauser, P. (1981) The Census of 1980. *Scientific American*, **245**, pp. 53–61.

Howells, J. R. L. (1984) The location of research and development: some observations and evidence from Britain. *Regional Studies*, **18**, 13–29.

Kondratieff, N. D. (1935) The long waves in economic life. *Review of Economic Statistics*, **17**, pp. 105–15.

Kuznets, S. S. (1930) *Secular Movements in Production and Prices*. New York: Houghton Mifflin.

Kuznets, S. S. (1940) Schumpeter's business cycles. *American Economic Review*, **30**, pp. 250–71.

Kuznets, S. S. (1946) *National Product since 1869*. New York: National Bureau of Economic Research (Publications, No. 46).

Kuznets, S. S. (1966) *Modern Economic Growth: Rate, Structure and Spread*. New Haven and London: Yale University Press.

Lloyd, P. E. and Mason, C. M. (1978) Manufacturing industry in the inner city: a case study of Manchester. *Institute of British Geographers, Transactions, N.S.*, **3**, pp. 60–90.

Malecki, E. J. (1980*a*) Corporate organization of R and D and the location of technological activities. *Regional Studies*, **14**, pp. 219–34.

Malecki, E. J. (1980*b*) Science and technology in the American urban system, in Brunn, S. D. and Wheeler, J. O. (eds.) *The American Metropolitan System: Past and Future*. London: Edward Arnold.

Malecki, E. J. (1981*a*) Public and private sector interrelationships, technological change, and regional development. *Papers of the Regional Science Association*, **47**, pp. 161–38.

Malecki, E. J. (1981*b*) Government-funded R&D: some regional economic implications. *Professional Georgrapher*, **33**, pp. 72–82.

Mandel, E. (1975) *Late Capitalism*. London: Verso.

Mandel, E. (1980) *Long Waves of Capitalist Development*. Cambridge: Cambridge University Press.

Marshall, A. (1920) *Principles of Economics*. London: Macmillan.

Markusen, A. (1984) *Profit Cycles, Oligopoly and Regional Development*. Cambridge, Mass: M.I.T. Press.

Martin, J. E. (1966) *Greater London: An Industrial Geography*. London: Bell.

Massey, D. and Meegan, R. (1982) *The Anatomy of Job Loss*. London: Methuen.

Mensch, G. (1979) *Stalemate in Technology: Innovations overcome the Depression.* Cambridge, Mass: Ballinger.

Neil, A. (1983) The information revolution. *The Listener*, 23 June.

Oakey, R. P., Thwaites, A. T. and Nash, P. A. (1980) The regional distribution of innovative manufacturing establishments in Great Britain. *Regional Studies*, **14**, pp. 235–53.

Phillips, B. *et al.* (1983) Western Corridor: a special report. *The Times*, 30 June.

Rothwell, R. (1982) The role of technology in industrial change: implications for regional policy. *Regional studies*, **16**, pp. 361–9.

Rostow, W. W. (1978) Regional change in the fifth Kondratieff upswing, in Perry, D. C. and Watkins, A. J. (eds.) *The Rise of the Sunbelt Cities (Urban Affairs Annual Reviews*, **14**). Beverly Hills and London: Sage.

Saxenian, A. (1981) Silicon chips and spatial structure: The industrial basis of urbanization in Santa Clara Valley, California. University of California, Berkeley, Institute of Urban and Regional Development, Working Paper 345.

Schumpeter, J. A. (1939, 1982) *Business Cycles: A Theoretical, Historical and Statistical Account of the Capitalist Process.* (2 Volumes). New York and London: McGraw Hill. Reprinted Philadelphia: Porcupine Press.

Thomas, D. (1983) England's Golden West. *New Society*, 5 May.

van Duijn, J. J. (1983) *The Long Wave in Economic Life*. London: George Allen and Unwin.

Walker, M. (1982) The boom that's by-passing the new towns of Britain. *The Guardian*, 26 April.

Weinstein, B. L. and Firestine, R. E. (1978) *Regional Growth and Decline in the United States: The Rise of the Sunbelt and the Decline of the Northeast*. New York: Praeger.

Wise, M. J. (1951) On the evolution of the jewellery and gun quarters in Birmingham. *Institute of British Geographers, Transactions and Papers*, **15**, pp. 57–72.

2

The Genesis
of Silicon Valley

ANNALEE SAXENIAN

*How did the Silicon Valley phenomenon
come about? What circumstances encouraged
electronics and related firms to settle
there in ever-increasing numbers? What were the effects
of this single-industry boom on the area?*

In 1940, Santa Clara County was a peaceful agricultural valley. In the
early 1950s a few fledgling electronics firms located in the county. As
the industry began to take root, it became one of the fastest growing
urban areas in the United States. By 1970 the region had gained
international fame as Silicon Valley, the capital of the semiconductor
industry and the densest concentration of 'high technology' enterprises in the world. This paper examines the dynamics underlying the
accelerated transformation of this California region.

Santa Clara County lies at the southern tip of San Francisco Bay.
About 1312 square miles in size, it encompasses a valley flanked by
low mountains of the Coastal Range. The valley itself constitutes
approximately one-third of the total area of the county, or about 436
square miles (see figure 2.1). From the time of its settlement by the
Spanish colonizers in the late 1700s, an agrarian economy was highly
successful in this fertile valley. Intensive agricultural development
was undertaken in Santa Clara County throughout the late nineteenth
and early twentieth centuries. By 1940, the region had developed into
a fully integrated agricultural community, boasting about 100,000
acres of orchards, 8000 acres of more traditional vegetable crops and
over 200,000 food processing plants. At that time, the county was
ranked as one of the fifteen most productive agricultural counties in
the country and it accounted for one-third of California's annual crop
of plums, cherries, pears, and apricots (Belser, 1970). It is remembered
by old-timers as a bucolic agricultural haven.

The city of San Jose was the largest of nine incorporated juris-
dictions in the county. With a population of 68,000, it was the county

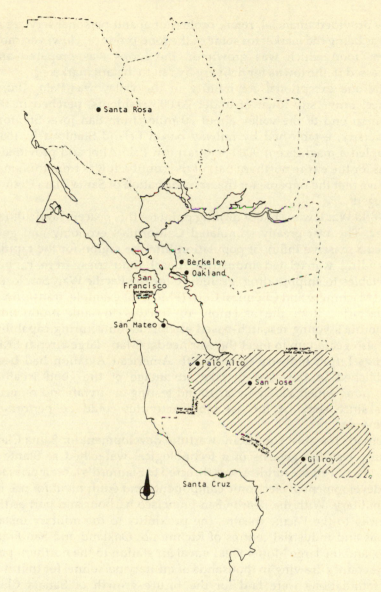

Figure 2.1 Santa Clara County in the context of the San Francisco Bay region.

seat and the centre for agricultural processing, packaging and distribution for the region. It boasted a diverse collection of canneries, food machinery industries and supportive businesses and services. The other towns scattered throughout the lush Santa Clara Valley were, with one exception, small urban pockets of less than 5000 population, which acted as service centres for the surrounding agricultural fields.

They provided financial, retail, professional and personal services as well as being the market for some of the food produce. However, most of the food which was grown on the farms was prepared and processed in the towns for delivery by rail to distant markets.

The one exceptional community in the valley was Palo Alto, a genteel university town of under 20,000 residents, perched in the northern end of the valley about 20 miles from San Jose. Stanford University, established by railway baron Leland Stanford in 1885, occupied a magnificent 9000-acre farm in Palo Alto, and provided a focus for the entire northern part of the county. It was from this small enclave that the impetus for the transformation of Santa Clara County emerged.

World War II was a major turning point for this peaceful agricultural valley. The war greatly stimulated California's economy and generated a massive influx of population into the region for the rapidly expanding war-related industries. Local industries, from canned vegetables to shipbuilding, geared up for the Pacific War. San Jose's Food Machinery and Chemical Corp (FMC), for example, transformed its factories from the assembly of tractors to tank production. California's young research-based aircraft manufacturing capability was also geared up to meet the war needs. (Many large aircraft firms such as Litton Industries and North American Aviation had been established in the state to take advantage of the good weather conditions which allowed year-round testing of aircraft and reduced costs since some of the assembly activities could be performed outdoors.)

Perhaps the most significant wartime development for Santa Clara County was the genesis of a technological watershed at Stanford University. Federal funding was directed to Stanford's laboratories for the development of electronic components and equipment for use by the military. With the nearby San Francisco harbour and port as the gateway to the Pacific theatre, the proximity to the military installations and industrial centres of Richmond, Oakland and San Francisco, and the large Moffet Field naval air station in the northern part of the county drawing in thousands of military personnel for training, the foundations were laid for the future growth of Sanata Clara County.

As the Second World War drew to a close, events in Santa Clara County began to pick up momentum. The population swelled with the influx of returning military personnel who passed through the Bay area en route to posts in the Pacific.

Frederick Terman, a far-sighted and ambitious electrical engineering professor at Stanford (later to become dean, provost and Vice President) returned to the region from administering a major military project at Harvard, determined to improve the university's then primitive electrical engineering programme. He actively sought government and business funding for this purpose, with the promise that it would bring new indigenous industry to the West to balance its agricultural resources. He contended that universities needed to develop a new relationship with the new genre of science- and technology-based industries which were dependent upon brain-power as their main resource. Terman spoke of the 'community of interest between the University and local industry' and consciously cultivated a 'community of technical scholars' in Palo Alto. As he described it,

Such a community is composed of industries using highly sophisticated technologies, together with a strong university that is sensitive to the creative activities of the surrounding industry. This pattern appears to be the wave of the future. (Bernstein, *et al.*, 1977).

Terman's success in this is clear. In 1955, gifts from corporations to Stanford had reached half a million dollars annually; by 1965, they exceeded $2 million; and in 1976 they had reached $6.9 million. Most importantly for the development of the local electronics industry, through Terman's careful attention to faculty building, Stanford rapidly attained the reputation as one of the two best electrical engineering programmes in the country (along with MIT).

The war-related aerospace and electronics enterprises which lo-cated in Santa Clara County clustered their operations in the north around the university. The initial precedent for this was set by the county's pre-war electronics companies. Hewlett-Packard Co began operations in a small garage shop in Palo Alto in 1938. In 1942, the Varian brothers pioneered the klystron tube (the foundation of modern radar and microwave communications) in the Stanford laboratories, and subsequently established their firm, Varian Associ-ates, nearby. In addition, the Stanford Research Institute (SRI) was founded in 1946 at Stanford University. SRI had a broad charter which emphasized performing research to help stimulate West Coast busi-ness (SRI International, 1980).

The outbreak of the Korean War and the ensuing 'Cold War' period guaranteed a continuing flow of funds to Stanford and firms in the area for basic electronics research and development, as well as creating a large and identifiable demand for new high-technology electronic products. The development of the ballistic missile system, in par-ticular, dramatically boosted the West Coast aircraft and missile industries, creating a large and guaranteed demand for prototype components from the young semiconductor industry. During this period, most of the local aircraft firms diversified themselves into production for the space industry. Terman reportedly used the government and academic contacts he had made during the war to attract a large proportion of the Pentagon's research and procurement dollars to the Stanford area. Between 1950 and 1954, military prime contracts awarded to California totalled about $13 billion, or 14 per cent of all such awards nationwide.

During the 1940s and 1950s a number of already well-established electrical- and electronics-related firms also moved operations into Santa Clara County to take advantage of the proximity to the war-related aircraft, missile and aerospace markets. Sylvania, Fairchild Camera and Instrument, General Electric, Philco-Ford, Westinghouse, Itel, and Kaiser all established manufacturing branch plants in the county.

Some large national firms also located research and development facilities in the county during this period. The biggest and most important of all was the research facility of the aerospace giant Lockheed, which was founded in the Stanford Industrial Park in 1956. IBM established a research centre in San Jose in 1952. ITT, Admiral and Sylvania also set up R&D laboratories in the county.

The development of the Stanford Industrial Park in the early 1950s represented the culmination of Terman's vision of an academy-industry partnership. It was one of the first industrial parks in the country, and Terman called it 'our secret weapon'. Established on 660 acres of land adjoining the Stanford Campus, leases in the park were granted only to high-technology firms which might be beneficial to Stanford University (Blakeslee, 1977). The leases were granted for ninety-nine years, and the seventy-five resident firms now pay minimal rent – enough to cover property taxes alone.

The industrial park also provided a model for landscaping and set the physical standards for subsequent high-technology industry in Santa Clara County. Factories and research buildings were made to resemble low-lying campus buildings and to convey the image of clean, modern and innovative industry. As one observer noted,

> No sooty smokestacks or shabby old factories mar the scenery. The science companies for the most part operate in sleek modern buildings in fifty-one verdant industrial parks, which provide a campus-like setting for research and manufacturing (Bylinsky, 1974).

A pattern of industrialization was thus consolidated in Santa Clara County during the decade following World War II which provided the underpinnings for the future burgeoning of electronics and semiconductor enterprises in the area. While the war stimulated the region's economy and subsequently the development of aerospace and electronics production and research in the region, Stanford's engineering school had begun to provide a substantial supply of high calibre scientists and engineers. By the mid-1950s the region was distinguished by a rich and supportive educational and technological milieu consisting of high-quality universities, research institutions and older technology-based firms. Santa Clara County had become an ideal environment for innovative, science-based industry.

The region's most dynamic growth phase was associated with the birth of a revolutionary new industry, the semiconductor industry. In 1955, William Shockley established Santa Clara County's first semiconductor firm. Shockley, one of the three original inventors of the transistor, returned to Palo Alto from Bell Laboratories to establish Shockley Transistor Company. He thus established one of the original spin-offs, in an industry that came to be characterized by this defection process. In 1957, eight of Shockley's best scientists in turn broke off themselves and gained financial backing from Fairchild Camera and Instrument to start their own firm. By 1965, ten new Santa Clara County semiconductor firms had spun-off from Fairchild, and the Santa Clara Valley had replaced Boston as the centre of gravity for new electronic firm locations. Between 1959 and 1979, Fairchild Semiconductor spawned an amazing total of fifty new companies in the county. Virtually every established semiconductor firm in the valley can trace its genealogy back at least indirectly to roots at Fairchild.

By the mid-1950s, Santa Clara County had already become one of the best possible locations in the country for the formation and growth of new semiconductor firms. The region's two distinguishing characteristics were the unusually large supply of scientific and engineering manpower coming out of the universities, research institutions and laboratories in the area, and the huge market for semiconductors generated by the defence and aerospace contracts and subcontracts directed to the region. Stanford University was also extremely responsive to the needs of companies in the area. Finally, once a few firms like Fairchild had succeeded, there was easy access to venture capital for the founding and expansion of new firms in the area due to the county's proximity to San Francisco, the financial centre of the West (Mutlu, 1979).

An indication of Santa Clara County's bountiful supply of scientific and engineering manpower is the rapidly increasing number of advanced degrees granted in electrical engineering by the local universities. Between 1950 and 1954, Stanford awarded 67 doctoral degrees in electrical engineering, between 1960 and 1964 it awarded 185, and for 1970 to 1974, 242. Meanwhile, the University of California at Berkeley awarded 19, 72 and 202 for the same time perods (Mutlu, 1979).

In the early 1960s, the number of PhDs granted yearly by Stanford exceeded the number granted by MIT. Since 1960, U.C. Berkeley and Stanford combined were granting yearly twice as many PhDs as MIT in electrical engineering (Mutlu, 1979). This large supply of university graduates made it easier for small firms in the area to recruit engineers. It also provided a larger pool of potential entrepreneurs, as most new semiconductor firms were started by university PhDs and faculty members.

Local research institutions (SRI and NASA's Ames Research Center) and the R&D laboratories of the older electronics firms (especially IBM, ITT, Admiral and Sylvania) and major aerospace contractors (Litton Industries, Lockheed, Westinghouse, General Telephone, Intel, Kaiser Industries, Philco-Ford, General Electric and Precision Equipment) all recruited engineers nationally, thus providing an even larger supply of high calibre engineering manpower for small new firms to draw upon. Quite often these small firms were able simply to steal top employees from the larger firms. As the electronic component in aerospace and military products increased, the number of engineers employed in these firms grew dramatically. Lockheed, for example, employed a full 2200 research scientists in 1962 (Mutlu, 1979). In sum, significant external economies had been created in the Santa Clara Valley which benefited small semiconductor companies with respect to manpower sources. No other area in the United States provided such a rich concentration of technologically skilled labour.

The most decisive factor underlying the initial rapid growth of semiconductor firms in Santa Clara County was the amount of government spending directed to the region. The government market for electronics in California grew steadily after World War II until the state's share of military and space markets for semiconductors was greater than any other state in the country. The prior concentration of aircraft and aerospace firms gave California a significant edge over all other parts of the country, as the main customers for young semiconductor firms during this period were military prime contractors and their subcontractors. (Even Massachusetts lacked the concentration of major aerospace contactors which Santa Clara County possessed.)

As the semiconductor component of missiles and defence systems grew, and their complexity increased, a premium was put on the spatial proximity of the semiconductor firm to its electronic subsystem prime contractors. The need for interaction and collaboration between aerospace firms and their semiconductor producing subcontractors grew rapidly as the complexity of integrated circuits increasingly required custom-made designs. Spatial proximity between the components manufacturers and the subsystem producers economized on

R&D personnel and time, and reduced communication costs. Since most semiconductor firms were very small in the 1960s, they had limited ability to interact over long distances. Thus those new firms which located close to prime contractors and subsystem manufacturers had a definite advantage over other small firms located further away.

Throughout the years of the Second World War, military prime contracts to the Pacific Region totalled $25.5 billion annually, or 12.3 per cent of the total awarded in the United States. During the Korean War years, the share going to the region had grown to 17.9 per cent of the total nationwide, or $17 billion annually. By 1961, the Pacific region led the country with 27.5 per cent of the total military prime contract awards (Bacon and Rempp, 1967). These awards included a rapidly increasing amount of semiconductors. During the 1960s California received 20 per cent of all defence-related prime contracts of $10,000 or more and 44 per cent of all National Aeronautics and Space Administration (NASA) subcontract awards. By that time, 15–20 per cent of the cost of an aircraft was accounted for by electronic equipment, and at least 30 per cent of missile systems was accounted for by electronics (Mutlu, 1979).

Finally, the Pacific region received an overwhelming share of federal R&D obligations. In 1964 it topped the nation with 36.5 per cent of all Defense Department R&D expenditures and 47.5 per cent of all NASA R&D obligations. The region also received 23.0 per cent of all Atomic Energy R&D obligations (Bacon and Rempp, 1967).

Stanford's activities played a significant, though secondary, role in drawing new firms to the county during this period. The programmes provided by Stanford included the honours programme, whereby employees of local companies could attend the university during evenings or on company time in order to obtain advanced degrees in science and engineering; and a cooperative programme of industry-university research sharing and seminars. By 1961, there were already thirty-two companies participating in the honours programme, with approximately 400 employees attending courses at the university. Such programmes were invaluable for small firms and their employees in an industry characterized by rapidly changing technology and dependent upon highly qualified R&D personnel. While larger firms, such as AT&T with Bell Labs, had the resources to provide graduate level training in science and technology for their employees, for the small companies that dominated the young semiconductor industry, proximity to a university was crucial.

The Stanford Industrial Park was also seminal in encouraging new company formation in the county. The ready availability of space and facilities assisted small new firms with limited resources. By 1961, the park already housed twenty-five high-technology firms with a total employment of nearly 11,000. Later, other communities in the area also established industrial parks, which further enhanced company formation and growth in the region.

During its first decades, local industry was also liberally financed with venture capital. Once Fairchild had succeeded, financial support for new and expanding firms was easily obtained. The San Francisco milieu consisted of a large pool of wealthy individuals and families with discretionary incomes, and management consulting houses which provided advice and evaluative services. Of course, it had all the services and assets which proximity to a major financial centre provides to local business.

Small new semiconductor firms thus flourished in Santa Clara County during the 1950s and 1960s. Propelled by the combined force of agglomeration and the industry's rapid growth, the county soon achieved the reputation as Silicon Valley, the densest concentration of electronics and semiconductor companies and highly skilled technological talent in the world.

By the mid-1960s the composition of markets had changed and military demand had declined significantly in importance relative to the newer computer and industrial markets, but the original concentration of semiconductor production in the county acted as a powerful centripetal force for the continued clustering of new semiconductor and electronics firms. An enlarged supply of manpower, specialized inputs and services, and a social, cultural and educational environment which was particularly appropriate to semiconductor production had been generated by a decade of prior spatial concentration by the industry. Thus virtually all spin-off firms chose to locate only a short distance from parent companies in the county and older firms continued to expand production locally.

As the industry grew, local education institutions instituted programmes to meet the specific needs of the local firms. University of California, Berkeley and Stanford expanded their master's degree and PhD programmes, and many community colleges and vocational schools in the area instituted engineering and training programmes. Santa Clara College, for example, provides courses in semiconductor production technology. A study of San Jose's junior college system in its formative years reported that more than half of all job placements for graduates were as electronics technicians in the industrial and service sectors of the county economy (Keller, 1979). In short, the educational system was shaped to meet the occupational needs of the local economy.

Industrial growth also induced massive immigration into the county. With under 200,000 people in 1940, the population of Santa

Clara County more than doubled between 1950 and 1960, and then had nearly doubled again by 1970 when it surpassed the one million mark (see table 2.1). Well over 75 per cent of this growth was due to immigration, much of it being workers displaced by mechanization of agriculture, along with newly arrived immigrants from Mexico and Asia (Santa Clara County Planning Dept, 1980). Thus there was a substantial and growing supply of unskilled labour available for production in the industry.

Table 2.1 Population growth and components of increase: Santa Clara County, California 1940–1980.

Year	Total Population	Interval	Total increase Number	Per Cent	Components Natural increase	Net immigration
1940	175,000	1940–1950	115,500	66.8	n.a.	n.s.
1950	290,500	1950–1960	351,815	121.1	23%	77%
1960	642,315	1960–1970	442,998	65.8	28%	72%
1970	1,065,313	1970–1980	184,687	17.3	57%	43%
1980	1,250,000					

Source: County of Santa Clara Planning Department (1980) *Components of Yearly Population Increase, 1950–1979, Santa Clara County*, INFO No. 660.

Supplies of specialized inputs and services were also guaranteed in Santa Clara County as a result of prior concentration of the industry. A variety of local firms had been established to produce the photomasks, testing jigs, chemicals, silicon and special production equipment essential to manufacturing semiconductors. Many of these inputs were not easily available elsewhere in the country. Providing all these inputs and services in-house would have been either impossible or excessively costly for small new firms. Even the larger firms benefited from taking advantage of the lower costs due to the economies of scale in producing inputs or services to so many firms. Infrastructure and transportation networks had all been well established in the county, thus ensuring efficient and uninterrupted air service, easy transfer of products to the airport, supplies of energy and water and the necessary sewage facilities.

The creation of a milieu which was highly conducive to interfirm communication, information transfer and personnel mobility was an equally important form of localization economies. In an industry marked by rapid technological change, pervasive inter-company diffusion of ideas and severe competitive pressures which demanded always staying at the 'leading edge' of technology, there were clear benefits to spatial proximity and the clustering of firms. Small firms especially benefited, giving the frequency of product copying, second sourcing, and pirating of information and personnel in the industry. There was also an unusually high degree of interaction between employees of rival firms in Santa Clara County. Many were close personal friends and had gone to school together or worked together in the past, and much information, brainstorming and gossip were exchanged over the telephone or at the local 'watering holes'. Stanford's education and seminar programmes and the activities of newly formed industry associations with headquarters in the area further encouraged this interchange.

Santa Clara County companies also found it very easy to attract top scientists and engineers from all over the country to the 'Santa Clara scientific community'. Once the county had attained the status as the seat of all knowledge and the hotbed of technology for the semi-conductor industry, ambitious young scientists in the field invariably wanted to land jobs or start their own firms in the county.

Through social interaction, these young professionals also created a social and cultural milieu in the valley which provided a highly desirable lifestyle for these scientists. The social status and desir-ability of the area should not be underestimated as a factor in the continued success of the industry in Santa Clara County. Scientists, executives and managers all have stressed the sentiments of this observer,

> It's particularly pleasant place to live and work – a beautiful landscape of hills and plains, a bounteous garden of nature where fruit trees and wild flowers bloom even in February . . . Few places on earth so agreeably mix hedonistic delights with the excitement of urbanity . . . It enjoys mild winters, fog-free summers and a balmy spring and fall. Outdoor sports and recreation are year-round attractions . . . The area boasts 4000 PhDs . . . There are also at least 12,000 horses, some kept by those PhDs right on their home acreages, which are often within minutes of work. And within an hour's drive are the shops, restaurants, and cultural offerings of San Francisco (Bylinsky, 1974).

The social status of living among other PhDs and horse owners and the country's recreational opportunities and suburban lifestyle helped to draw the professional engineers and scientists who are so key to semiconductor production.

Agglomeration economies thus insured continued clustering of the proliferation of new semiconductor firm start-ups. In one year alone (1968) thirteen new spin-off enterprises originated in Santa Clara County. The pace continued through the first half of the 1970s. Outside the fertile environment which had been created in the region, many of these fledgling firms would never have survived. By 1970, five of the seven largest semiconductor firms in the United States had their

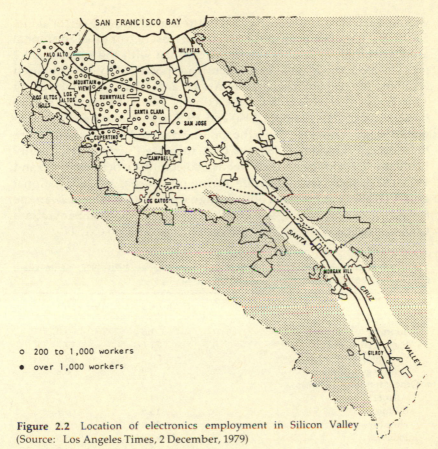

o   200 to 1,000 workers
•   over 1,000 workers

Figure 2.2 Location of electronics employment in Silicon Valley
(Source: Los Angeles Times, 2 December, 1979)

main facilities in Silicon Valley, and clustered around them was the
largest concentration of electronic communications, laser, microwave,
computer, advanced instrument and equipment manufacturers in the
world (figure 2.2).

As the electronics and semiconductor industries boomed, so too did
the regional economy. Between 1950 and 1975, the population of Santa
Clara County increased by over one million people. The pace of
population growth in the region far surpassed growth rates for
California and for the United States as a whole. The population of
the county grew 121 per cent during the 1950s, while California's
population grew 48.5 per cent and the US population grew only 18.5
per cent. Likewise, during the following decade the county's population grew 66 per cent, while California's grew 27 per cent and that of
the United States only 13.3 per cent.

Total employment in the county nearly doubled between 1940 and
1950, and more than doubled again between 1950 and 1960. In twenty

years, over 60,000 jobs were created in the manufacturing sector alone. Each new manufacturing job generated at least two or three additional jobs. This high multiplier stands in contrast with the estimated 1.2 jobs created by a new manufacturing position in the matured economy of the San Francisco Bay Area (Santa Clara County Housing Task Force, 1977). More than 400,000 new jobs were created during these two decades. Between 1960 and 1975, the county's employment grew 156 per cent, three times the national rate of 46 per cent and more than double California's 65 per cent increase (Santa Clara County Economic Development – Job Needs Project, 1978). Between 1970 and 1975, the growth rate for manufacturing jobs surpassed such national growth leaders as Houston and Orange County (see table 2.2). In the forty-year period from 1940 to 1980, total employment in Santa Clara County thus grew almost 1000 per cent, from 59,900 to 651,500.

Table 2.2 Manufacturing employment: percentage change 1970–1977: Santa Clara County, other metropolitan areas, and the United States.

	1970–1975	1975–1977
California	−1.6	6.0
Santa Clara County	21.6	10.7
Orange County	20.4	10.1
San Diego County	5.9	−0.8
Other Metropolitan Areas		
Atlanta	−4.7	−0.7
Boston	−15.6	6.1
Houston	20.0	7.8
Phoenix	−4.5	5.8
Seattle	9.9	4.9
United States	−8.8	5.6

Source: Santa Clara County Economic Development – Job Needs Project (1978) *Training and Jobs: Ways to Reduce Unemployment in Santa Clara County.*

The explosive growth of the region's economy is also reflected in the dramatic increases in its manufacturing value-added and value of shipments. In the five years between 1967 and 1972 alone, value-added in manufacture grew 53 per cent from $1.9 billion to $2.9 billion, making Santa Clara County the third highest ranked metropolitan area in the state of California for manufacturing value-added (after the Los Angeles/Long Beach and the San Francisco/Oakland SMSAs) (Security Pacific National Bank, 1976). By 1977, Silicon Valley ranked sixteenth in the country in the dollar value of its manufacturing shipments, with an estimated total of $16 billion (Garcia, 1979).

Santa Clara County also quickly became one of the wealthiest counties in the nation. In 1969, median family income in the San Jose

SMSA (coterminous with Santa Clara County) was already the highest among all of California's SMSAs, and a full 30 per cent above the median family income for the United States (table 2.3). By 1977, per capita personal income in Santa Clara County was $8,632, while it was $7,909 for California and $7,019 for the United States as a whole (Security Pacific Bank, 1979).

Table 2.3. Median family income, 1969 and 1975: San Jose SMSA, California and the United States.

	1969	1975
Santa Clara County	$12,456	$18,500
California	10,732	14,069
United States	9,586	14,095

Source: US Bureau of the Census (1970) *Census of Population: 1970. California.* Washington, DC: US Government Printing Office.
Stanford Research Institute (1980) *The Mid-Peninsula in the 80s.* Palo Alto, CA: SRI International.

The rapid expansion and agglomeration of semiconductor production in Santa Clara County thus created a single industry boomtown. Today, at least one-third of Silicon Valley's workers are employed in the approximately 700 electronics-related companies in the region, while many of the remainder are in occupations which support or service this 'high-technology' complex.

References

Bacon, S. R. Jr and Rempp, K. A. (1967) *Electronics in Michigan.* Ann Arbor: University of Michigan, Institute of Science and Technology.

Belser, K. (1970) The making of suburban America. *Cry California,* 5 (4).

Bernstein, A., DeGrasse, B., Grossman, R., Paine, C. and Siegel, L. (1977) *Silicon Valley: Paradise or Paradox?* Mountain View, California: Pacific Studies Center.

Blakeslee, S. (1977) Want to develop a world center of innovative technology? It's simple. Get yourself a Fred Terman. *The Stanford Observer,* November.

Bylinsky, G. (1974) California's great breeding ground for industry. *Fortune,* 89, pp. 128–35.

Garcia, A. (1979) Silicon Valley seen shifting its emphasis. *Journal of Commerce,* 17 January.

Keller, J. (1979) *Industrialization, immigration and community formation in San Jose, California: social processes in the electronics industry.* Ann Arbor: University of Michigan.

Mutlu, S. (1979) *International and interregional mobility of industrial capital: the case of the American automobile and electronics companies.* Unpublished PhD thesis, University of California, Berkeley.

Santa Clara County Economic Development – Job Needs Project (1978) *Training and Jobs: Ways to reduce Unemployment in Santa Clara County*. San Jose: Santa Clara County Planning Department.

Santa Clara County Housing Task Force (1977) *Housing, a Call for Action*. San Jose: Santa Clara County Planning Department.

Santa Clara County Planning Department (1980) *Components of Yearly Population Increases, 1950–1979*. Info Fact Sheet 660. San Jose: Santa Clara County Planning Department.

Saxenian, A. (1981) *Silicon chips and spatial structure. The Industrial basis of urbanization in Santa Clara County, California*. University of California, Berkeley, Institute of Urban and Regional Development, Working Paper 345.

Security Pacific National Bank (1976) *Summary and Outlook for the State of California, 1940–1974*, San Francisco: Security Pacific National Bank.

Security Pacific National Bank (1979) *Monthly Summary of Business Conditions: Northern Coastal*. San Francisco: Security Pacific National Bank.

3

High-tech jobs, markets and economic development prospects: evidence from California

ANN R. MARKUSEN

What does the evidence of four studies
of high-tech industries in California tell
us about future employment, structural trends and
locational characteristics of these sectors of industry?

Public interest in subsidizing the high-tech route to economic development is predicated upon three basic assumptions about the links between such industries and economic performance. First, high-tech industries are expected to create substantial numbers of new jobs. Not only are these jobs badly needed to offset losses in older, mature manufacturing sectors, but it is anticipated that they will occur in relatively well-paid and stable occupational categories. Second, the high-tech industries are envisioned as composed of highly competitive, innovative firms, whose activities collectively will serve a 'seedbed' function for the economy at large [1]. Third, policies designed to subsidize high-tech industries assume that jobs and income so generated will accrue to the nation, region or community providing the incentive.

This chapter presents the first empirical evidence on these questions from four case studies of high-technology industries in California. The four studies – on biotechnology, computer software, photovoltaics, and robotics – were done for the state's Commission on Industrial Innovation in 1982 by academics at various California universities [2]. Each study draws together the evidence from the existing literature, what data are available from government and business sources, and the results of direct interviews with California firms in each sector. The evidence is somewhat unevenly developed across the set; for example, the biogenetics and software cases provide more data on locational tendencies than do the other two. Nevertheless, each case study provides answers unavailable elsewhere in the literature. Together, the case studies permit some tentative answers on the three issues and offer insights into the peculiarities and variation in growth prospects across these disparate sectors.

Job Creation and Labour Force Requirements

The four studies confirm that high-tech sectors offer rapid and significant job growth prospects. In the midst of an economy-wide recession in the early 1980s, these sectors experienced dramatic rates of job expansion, in some cases growing by more than 50 per cent per year. However, these gains were mounted on a relatively small job base; most of the studies found job gains will slow in the coming decade, approaching 5 to 10 per cent growth per year. Overall, the numbers of jobs anticipated in high-tech sectors do not appear sufficient to outweigh the job loss in other sectors of the economy. Furthermore, the studies suggest that the occupational, ethnic and gender composition of new jobs in high-tech sectors will tend to worsen the current trend toward the 'disappearing middle', that is toward a labour force bifurcated between high-paid professionals and low-paid service workers (Bluestone and Harrison, 1982).

Taken individually, the high-tech sectors studied here have posted high rates of new job creation in the past decade. Software, for instance, doubled in size over the 1970s, presently employing about 250,000 workers. The authors of the software study expect this number to grow to approximately 450,000 by 1990. After that date, two factors should stem job growth rates in software. First, sales in information processing are expected to level off at about 4 to 5 per cent of GNP, up from 2.5 per cent in 1981. Second, a shift away from labour-intensive software services towards software products (from 12 to 25 per cent of the market from 1980 to 1985 alone) and accompanying gains in productivity will drastically reduce the need for additional software engineers. It may even be the case that a surplus of such highly trained specialists will be the legacy of a successful software design era.

The photovoltaics sector, perhaps because it is younger, has a much more modest record of job creation. Photovoltaics output is growing at a remarkable pace. Shipments grew at 85 per cent per year in the period 1977–1981. But market growth is not paralleled by job growth, since productivity gains are rapidly reducing labout requirements. The authors of the photovoltaics study estimate that the number of workers needed to produce a unit of output will further fall by a factor of two to three in the future. At most, about 2400 employees are presently working on this technology. Coyle and Hawley expect these numbers to grow to 5000 nationally by 1990, and note that the gains could be much greater if the technique becomes commercially competitive with other forms of electricity generation. Of course, in the latter case, jobs in competing sectors such as coal, oil and nuclear could disappear as a consequence.

In biogenetics, the current job numbers are also quite modest. Some 5000 workers now produce synthetic genetic material, which represents a tenfold gain from the mid-1970s. This rapid rate of increase is also expected to taper off as large productivity gains occur; Feldman and O'Malley estimate that about 44,000 jobs will exist in 1990. Unlike the other sectors, where the authors studied only direct employment in the sector, the biogenetics group tried to estimate the jobs created in the supply sector associated with synthetic genetics. While they found it difficult to disaggregate specifically biogenetic supplies from conventional pharmaceutical and medical supplies, they generously estimated that less than 26,000 jobs currently exist in the support industry. The authors also emphasize that the creation of synthetic drugs will displace jobs in those sectors that currently make organic drugs such as insulin, just as synthetic fabrics and artificial rubber shifted jobs from one type of production process to another.

Robotics employment, like software, is perhaps more promising in terms of absolute numbers of jobs. From a current workforce of about 10,000, the robotics study estimates that the total robotics workforce will approach 100,000 by 1990. In addition, new jobs will be created in installation, maintenance and servicing of robots. However, many of these jobs will occur in the machine tools industry and simply represent job shifts from older generations of machine tools to new ones. And, as Dorf points out, some 440,000 workers will be replaced by robots by the end of the century, although many of these losses could be met by attrition or by allowing for retraining of operators for new positions. The net job-creating potential of robotics, however, will be considerably less than the gross figures and could conceivably be negative.

These job creation figures, whose tentative character is stressed by the authors of the studies, permit us a very speculative estimate of the overall job generation forthcoming from these four sectors. Excluding both additional jobs in support services and job displacement in downstream user industries, the studies suggest that about 600,000 total jobs will be available in these sectors in 1990, a more than doubling of present jobs. If we generously estimate total related support jobs generated at four times this direct job creation, the total number of high-tech jobs in these sectors would amount to about 3 million in 1990. While this is substantial, it pales in comparison with the estimated 25 million jobs needed to compensate for jobs expected to be displaced by high technology (Weiss, 1984). Furthermore, we know that the American labour force will continue to grow as more young people and women enter its ranks. If high-technology jobs cannot even meet the need for work created by redundancies, how can they be expected to provide opportunities for these new entrants? Or alternatively, will the burden of displacement fall inordinately on older, skilled blue-collar workers who have few options for career changes given competition from younger, cheaper, differentially educated workers?

The four studies also provide insights on the occupational composition of high-tech jobs. The percentages of professional-technical workers varies dramatically, from a high of 63 per cent in the case of the infant biogenetics industry to 30 per cent in software to even lower levels in robotics and photovoltaics. Biogenetics employs large proportions of specially trained biologists, chemists and other technicians. In two sectors, software and robotics, substantial numbers of engineers are required. One in three software employees is a computer specialist, and the study cites industry shortages of about 50,000 software engineers in the short run. Similarly, the robotics sector may require as many as 10,000 new manufacturing engineers in the next five years and, in the longer run, will generate user demands for mechanical engineers with software skills. These are the only significant labour shortages described in the four studies. And, as noted above, perfection of software packages and completion of robotic systems will most likely result in a longer-run decline in the demand for these types of engineers.

Only two of the sectors, photovoltaics and robotics, require skilled and/or semi-skilled assembly labour. The photovoltaics sector has as much as 50 per cent of its workforce in routine assembly occupations. Robotics employs substantial numbers of machinists in actual production of mechanical components and assembly. In contrast, the biogenetics sector has only 2 per cent of its workforce in production and another 2 per cent in maintenance.

All sectors require relatively high proportions of clerical and service workers. In the software sector, approximately two-thirds of all jobs are in low-paid clerical and service occupations. In biogenetics, 17 per cent of the jobs are in clerical roles. And in photovoltaics, 10 per cent of the jobs are office jobs with another 10 per cent in service occupations. As a residual, these sectors have relatively low management and sales workforces, often because researchers-turned-entrepreneurs must manage and market their highly specialized and custom-made innovations. As these sectors mature, we can expect the proportions in these latter categories to rise.

The evidence on current race and gender composition of the high-tech workforce is scanty in the studies. They tend, however, to confirm a growing specialization of workers in a highly bifurcated occupational structure. At the top are the professional/technical workers and management, largely white male and often quite young. Only in software were relatively large numbers of women employed as technicians, but they were under-represented in the more innovative, software design occupations. And it is software programmers who are most vulnerable to longer-term redundancies as user-friendly software packages are developed. The authors note that only in those cases of female entrepreneurship, i.e. when one or more owners or top-level managers of a firm were women, did women appear proportionately in the professional workforce. Professional/technical workers in these sectors appear to be disproportionately white.

In the 'middle', these sectors offer relatively few skilled blue-collar jobs. No mention of any such group is made in the software and biogenetics studies. Robotics is perhaps the only case where blue-collar machinists and mechanics will maintain jobs in substantial numbers. And, as elsewhere in the economy, these jobs will likely continue their extraordinarily high concentrations of men. Operative jobs in the photovoltaics sector are largely semi-skilled and unskilled, and therefore largely occupied by minority women. These are low-paid, high-turnover jobs.

The biotechnology study is the only one which offers an aggregate estimate of minority and women employment, with some breakdowns by occupation. The authors estimate that 41 per cent of biotechnology jobs are occupied by women, just about the average for the entire economy. Yet women are heavily over-represented in the clerical occupations in this sector, constituting 94 per cent of the clerical workforce. Women are under-represented in the professional and managerial categories, with 37 per cent of these jobs. And, the authors note, no inference of their place in the decision-making hierarchy can be made from these aggregate data. Minorities constitute 21 per cent of the biotechnology workforce, although the authors of the study caution that these figures are probably over-inflated due to the classification of foreign nationals as minorities in their survey. Much new research is needed to confirm whether or not the high-tech sectors will exacerbate the gender and race differentials which currently characterize the American workforce.

What can be affirmed from these studies is that the occupational structure of these high-tech sectors will contribute to the 'vanishing middle'. Small numbers of professional workers will enjoy higher incomes and exciting work, although in the longer run some of them will face dislocation as well. Large numbers of blue-collar workers economy-wide are apt to be displaced by the new technologies with new skilled-labour jobs in high-tech sectors too limited in number to compensate. The majority of new jobs created, especially in the longer run, will be in the lower-paid clerical, service and assembly occupations. These may offer job opportunities to women and minorities, yet without the income security and interesting work that is our vision of high-tech employment. And, to speculate for a moment, the pressure to increase productivity and profitability in these sectors may lead to displacement in these occupations as well, as assembly jobs are transported overseas and clerical work is replaced by more efficient word processors.

Industry Structure

The four studies confirm that considerable firm entry, exit and jockeying for position accompany the growth of high-tech sectors. In the short run, positive net rates of new firm formation promise to keep competition lively, although the presence and practices of large, diversified corporations loom as problematic in all four sectors in the longer run. Assessing competitive performance from quantitative indicators on numbers of firms, size of firms and concentration ratios is in an imperfect exercise, yet the evidence from the studies is both varied and insightful.

In terms of sheer numbers of competitors, the four sectors range from a very densely populated market of thousands of small firms (software) to a modest representation of 113 (biogenetics) to sparse populations of less than two dozen (robotics and photovoltaics). Within each, both large and small firms compete, but the average firm size varies dramatically. Both software and biogenetics have relatively small averages, of the order of about thirty employees. Photovoltaics and robotics, on the other hand, have a preponderance of relatively large firms.

These populations and average sizes are in flux. On the one hand, new entrants continue to challenge the industries' leaders, resulting in net additions to the absolute numbers of firms, markedly in software and biogenetics. The phenomenon of the spin-off – disgruntled, ambitious and enterprising engineers and scientists leaving an existing firm to set up their own competitors – does appear to explain robust rates of new firm formation.

On the other hand, new entrants are not always small firms, but may be large conglomerates who enter by buying out smaller firms and who bring powerful competitive weapons to bear on the market. In photovoltaics, for instance, large energy corporations with surplus capital from oil revenues have entered by absorbing small independents. Three of the top five photovoltaic firms are wholly-owned subsidiaries of oil companies; ARCO is the single largest competitor with as much as 40 per cent of this new market. In robotics, the two independent leaders have been challenged by the entry, in 1981 alone, of the following five conglomerates: General Electric, Westinghouse, IBM, United Technologies and Bendix. Similarly, in biogenetics, pharmaceutical and chemical corporations are actively pursuing buyouts of small pioneers. And, in software, there were fifty-seven mergers encompassing $244 million worth of assets in the first six months of 1981 alone.

The net result of these countervailing tendencies can be seen in the present degree of concentration in each industry. Concentration ratios measure the percentage of value added or shipments of an industry accounted for by the largest firms.[3] Of the four high-tech sectors studied here, three are highly concentrated. In robotics, two companies account for more than 50 per cent of market share. In photovoltaics, four firms control 86 per cent of the market. Even in biogenetics, where the average firm size is small, the four largest companies control 52 per cent of the market. Only in software are small firms dominant and concentration ratios low. No software company accounts for more than 5 per cent of the market, and small firms control about 80 per cent.

It is more difficult to gather data on changes in these ratios over time. Some argue that while existing rates of concentration are high, new entry may invigorate competition. Certainly in software, the available evidence suggests that this is the case; the proportion of the market controlled by the four largest firms actually dropped from 18 per cent in 1972 to 14 per cent in 1977. However, this sector may be unique. In both robotics and photovoltaics, where conglomerate entry is significant and where signs of excess capacity have already emerged (both studies cite utilization rates of only about 50 per cent), concentration may intensify. The share of the largest two or three corporations may be eroded, but the degree of concentration of market power in the largest eight and twenty firms may rise. In photovoltaics, for instance, Coyle and Hawley expect heightened competition among a dozen or so firms, but also expect some of the current fifteen competitors to fail. And even in software, Osborne *et al.* detected an increase in the share of plant accounted for by the very largest companies.

The industrial organization literature cautions against using concentration ratios as an accurate measure of degree of competition. There are two major problems, each tending to bias the results in opposite directions. First, the ratios are computed on the basis of domestic establishments and firms. Since they do not include foreign competitors, whose products may account for a significant share of the domestic market, they may understate the degree of effective competition. Second, the ratios sum over a number of separate submarkets which may be of either a spatial or a product nature. If significant market niches exist within an industry, and firms tend to compete only in one against a limited number of competitors, then the concentration ratio will overstate the degree of effective competition. Similarly, if markets are spatially segregated and firms really only compete in one region, then concentration is further understated by the ratio. These adjustments were relatively important in the industries which we studied, although in each case their significance varied.

With respect to international competition, all the studies document the presence of foreign competitors. In the case of software, the ability of the Japanese and Europeans to compete is believed to be seriously handicapped by language and cultural differences. Both biogenetics and photovoltaics sectors have international competitors, but these tend to be large multinational corporations whose successes might threaten US firms' market shares but would not necessarily alter the oligopolistic nature of those markets. The greatest international competition across the study set appears to be in robotics. Compared to only twenty firms in the United States, Dorf estimates that some forty European and one hundred and forty Japanese companies are competing to produce robotic parts and systems.

On the other hand, substantial product differentiation does appear to characterize all four industries. In robotics, for instance, only three independent firms have any significant share of the robot market, while four other companies are competing to design vision systems. In biogenetics, firms vie in highly specialized products lines – human insulin, for instance. The biogenetics sector will most likely evolve like the ethical drug industry, where only a very few firms compete in any one substance (Walker, 1971). The market options in photovoltaics are at this point much more speculative, since the critical question will be whether or not this energy source will be competitive with present grid mixes. At least one firm the authors studied was solely dependent for its current viability on government contracts for quite specialized purposes. To the extent that small, new firms succeed in this sector, the authors believe that they will be in related functions such as distribution, installation, specialty items and intermediate supplies. In software, the one sector which appears highly competitive, the authors of the study found very serious compartmentalization of submarkets. Often, a small firm will develop a simple programme for a specialized purpose – say dental office billings – and monopolize that market. In a large number of these markets, concentration is in reality quite severe. There are, of course, some highly competitive software segments, such as all-purpose editing and word processing packages.

Yet these are the segments which large hardware firms are eager to capture, and informants believe that a future shake-out will result in a relatively small number of successful competitors.

It is difficult to sum up these countervailing tendencies with any degree of precision. The rule-of-thumb in the industrial organization literature is that the underestimation of concentration resulting from market segmentation most likely outweighs the overestimation from excluding international competition. Yet in a world of increasingly intense competition from the secular increase in economic integration, this assumption may no longer hold. However, even if we acknowledge the effective role of international competition, there is little in these studies to suggest that the future of these sectors will not be dominated by oligopolistic firms and practices. A number of speculations from the studies on future trends in these industries underscores this conclusion.

First of all, as high-tech products become less experimental and more standardized, contests for market share will increasingly reward large-scale marketing and financial capabilities. This has clearly been the trend in the semiconductor and computer sectors, the eldest siblings of this generation of high-tech industries. Currently, the two largest independent semiconductor firms are struggling to prevent themselves from being swallowed up by the computer corporations who constitute their major clients. All of our studies stressed the pressure that small firms feel to join up with a larger organization who can supply sales, marketing, service and financial resources to help them penetrate national and international markets once their product is perfected.

Second, the entry of large conglomerate competitors into all four of these sectors has changed the nature of the game. Particularly in photovoltaics and robotics, these newer entrants are accused of cross-subsidizing below-profit production in order to secure a market share in the longer run. Small, under-capitalized companies find it very difficult to weather this period of predatory competition, since they have no access to internal sources of funds in the same manner. Thus they are often compelled to accept a buyout or merger.

Third, the acceleration of vertical integration within these sectors has also complicated competition. If monopoly or monopsony power exists at any point in the chain, it means that clients or suppliers may be subject to unfair pressures. Competition among independent software vendors may not be sufficient to outweigh the advantages that computer firms may have in tying or advising their customers to certain software products. Consumers may end up paying oligopolistic prices for computer services even if the immediate market appears to be well-populated and competitive.

The basic evidence, then, on present and future industry structure does not offer much hope that these sectors will remain highly competitive and small business dominated reservoirs in the economy. They will be characterized by vigorous competition within market segments, but the major competitors are apt to be large, conglomerate and multinational corporations, with smaller firms addressing market niches or operating as subcontractors to the larger firms. The type of competition will thus be oligopolistic, rather than purely competitive, where each contesting firm wields substantial market power and is highly sensitive to moves by competitors. We have no hard and fast evidence on the effect on innovation, price, employment and spatial distribution of this form of competition.[4] At least one of our studies (photovoltaics) stresses that smaller firms believe that domination of the market by large corporations will result in the retardation of innovation, in the predatory elimination of smaller firms through cross-subsidization, in errors and miscalculations from lack of expertise in the product line, and even in the suppression of cost-effective techniques because they would undercut profitability in substitute product lines, in this case oil. Evaluation of such claims lies outside of our present capabilities, but the spectre of oligopolistic dominance clearly invites further study.

Spatial Distribution of Employment

The studies reviewed in this article are regrettably brief on the issue of present and future spatial distribution of high-tech firms and jobs. Yet this pattern is essential to the plans of local, state and national policy-makers who contemplate high-tech industries as a route toward economic revival and development. For the national government, one issue is whether or not subsidies and protection for high-tech sectors will result in domestic job growth. Since multinational conglomerate corporations are involved in every sector studied here, could aid result in a quickening of dispersal of some jobs and production facilities overseas? And, on the domestic front, could underwriting of these sectors inadvertently worsen the present imbalance in regional growth rates? For state and local governments, the issues are similar. Can a state government engender high-tech industries in a manner which ensures that resulting employment gains reside within state boundaries? And within the state, can high-tech jobs be channelled toward areas of high unemployment and underutilized public sector capacity? What happens in cases, like Silicon Valley, where too much high-tech development has already provoked serious environmental problems, overcrowded housing and highways, and related industrial growth control movements?

The studies offer only patchy evidence on these issues. But what they do show is informative. First, all of them confirm that current plant and job patterns are highly concentrated in a very few states. In biogenetics, half of all firms are located in California or Massachusetts. Employment is somewhat less concentrated, although 30 per cent of all synthetic genetics jobs are in California. In software, California accounts for 20 per cent of all jobs and an even higher percentage of firms. The authors of both studies expect these concentrations to continue; the software authors have forecast the continued pre-eminence and even improvement of the leading state, California, in its share of jobs. Photovoltaics is currently heavily concentrated in the arc of states from California to Texas. While California dominates the overall set, some East Coast locations, particularly Boston and the Philadelphia/New York/New Jersey area are also heavy competitors. And robotics, the production of which takes place in the traditional machining sector, can be found in some older manufacturing centres like Detroit, where it is linked with the auto industry, as well as in the newer high-tech centres.

The tendency to agglomerate seems to be related to three sets of factors. First, the historic links between these sectors and earlier sectors, such as micro-electronics and aerospace industries, seems to have anchored them early in their current locations. This is particularly true of the software and photovoltaic sectors, whose sites in the Boston area, Califonia and Texas are directly linked to computer manufacture and space programmes respectively. Second, all the sectors require pools of highly skilled professional and technical workers, who in addition to being spawned by the above-mentioned sectors are also associated with the presence of a good university. And finally, lifestyle issues which encompass urban, cultural, environmental, and recreational amenities are often essential to the maintenance of a satisfied professional workforce.

The tendency to disperse has been detected in some of our sectors. But it is important to note that dispersion almost always applies to specialized portions of the sectors' workforce, which are associated with the more routine production tasks or downstream marketing and service functions. For instance, software firms increasingly create sales, training, and servicing branches in cities across the country (and internationally) where their users are located. As software packages become a larger share of this market, this decentralization should intensify. Although both biogenetics and photovoltaics firms showed high degrees of inertia, the authors of both studies predicted that a limited impetus to decentralization would emerge in the desire to penetrate new markets. One photovoltaics firm has licensed its process to a Japanese firm for production in that country. Again, the more standardized the product, the greater this tendency.

Despite these tendencies, the studies stress the intentions of existing firms to maintain their managerial and developmental activities in present agglomerations. In a few cases, associated jobs might be decentralized, as programmers work at home or satellites permit transcontinental sales and service, but even in software, firms interviewed believed that face-to-face encounters are necessary to both research and sales efforts. Occasionally, a case of multinational decentralization of research can be detected, as in biogenetics, where some companies are contemplating opening European branches to tap new pools of researchers. In a related sector, one large semiconductor firm has recently set up a research establishment in Israel, where engineers and computer experts receive salaries of the order of one-third less than their American counterparts. Perhaps this trend will accelerate in the future, but the current expectation is that existing high-tech centres will maintain and expand their high-tech labour force. These early regional centres may actually increase their share of national professional/technical workers, although their overall shares of high-tech workers may decline, as sales, service and production jobs are dispersed. This suggests that late starters in the high-tech competition have handicaps in attracting the best-paid, most interesting high-tech jobs for their communities.

Within existing high-tech regions, several interesting trends can be detected. First of all, the proliferation of high-tech establishments is clearly passing by the older inner cities where the highest rates of unemployment are concentrated. Both Silicon Valley and Route 128 around Boston are newly developed, auto-based, suburban areas whose jobs and tax base do not overlay the inner-city poor not the central-city jurisdiction. The robotics study predicts few inner-city job increases. The software study shows that only large-scale data processing plants, which employ large numbers of minority women and can use existing industrial space in the inner city, have chosen to locate in places like West Oakland. The software researchers found that small software firms are very self-conscious about their 'address'. While other factors – lower cost labour and cheaper rents – might make inner-city centres attractive, these firms eschewed an Oakland or Richmond mailing address.

Thus, the ability of both inner cities and high-tech poor regions to attract new activity and the desirability of these new jobs created must be viewed with pessimism. The leading high-tech centres may be relieved to know that their competitive edge will not soon deteriorate. Ironically, however, it is precisely these areas where high-tech industries have become problematic. The software study noted that nine of the firms interviewed stated explicitly that housing shortages and/or transportation problems in the Bay Area made remaining there increasingly difficult (Saxenian, 1981). Within Silicon Valley, both at the county and city level, industrial growth controls including short-term moratoriums on new plants and density limits on numbers of employees per acre have been adopted. This remarkable phe- nomenon – communities claiming that they have had *too much* industrial growth – must be taken into account by policymakers at state or national levels whose plans could exacerbate the growth of high-tech industries in their contemporary locations and worsen the quality of life for their residents.

Summary

This review of the case studies on the three issues of jobs, industry structure and geographical tendencies of high-tech sectors leaves us with plenty of unanswered questions. In general, the results suggest that while substantial new jobs will emerge from these sectors, they may not be sufficient to counterbalance the decline of jobs in other sectors which are shrinking independently or directly in consequence of the new technologies. And, the dramatic gains and labour shortages registered at present will diminish and may perhaps reverse once products and services are fully designed and innovated. Furthermore, these new jobs will not counteract the long-term decline in blue-collar skilled occupations which have formed a core of the labour force in the past. Nor are women and minorities apt to participate proportionately in the better paid, more interesting jobs created. The review of industry trends suggests that the future structure of each of these sectors will consist of either multinational and conglomerate firms dominating the market or smaller companies monopolizing highly differentiated market niches. Finally, the limited spatial evidence in the studies suggests that existing high-tech centres will continue to dominate headquarters and research activities, often creating severe congestion problems in these regions, while outlying areas will be able to attract only the low-paid production activities, to the extent that there are any, and the normal sales and service functions which follow an industry's clients.

Acknowledgement

The author would like to thank her co-authors on the computer software project for their insights into high-tech industry issues over the research effort: Peter Hall, Barbara Wachsman, and Richard Osborn. Special thanks go to Marc Weiss, Deputy Director of the Commission on Industrial Innovation, for his comments on this summary. The studies reviewed here were all funded by the Commission, although the findings and recommendations do not necessarily represent the views of the Commission. The Institute of Urban and Regional Development provided excellent staff support for this effort.

Notes

1 Studies by Birch (1979) and Teitz *et al.* (1981) in recent years have underscored the disproportionately large share of new job creation accounted for by small businesses.
2 The studies covered are Coyle, Eugene B. and Hawley, James P.: *Photovoltaics: Technology for Energy Independence;* Dorf, Richard C.: *Robotics and Computer-Aided Manufacturing/Design: Keys to Increasing Productivity;* Osborn, Richard, Wachsman, Barbara, Markusen, Ann and Hall, Peter: *Computer Services, the People behind the Machines;* and Feldman, Marshall and O'Malley, Becky: *Biogenetics.* All were published in 1982 by the California Commission on Industrial Innovation and are available from the Department of Business and Economic Development, Sacramento.
3 Concentration ratios as indicators of degree of market power are the subject of heated debate. Scherer (1980) and Mueller (1970) conclude that they probably underestimate market power more often than overestimating it. The more disaggregated the sector, the greater the degree of concentration detected.
4 Many studies in the industrial organization tradition have been critical of the innovative performance of large, oligopolistic corporations. See, for example, the discussions in Mansfield (1968) and Scherer (1980).

References

Birch, David (1979) *The Job Generation Process.* Cambridge, Mass: MIT Program on Neighbourhood and Regional Change.

Bluestone, Barry and Harrison, Bennett (1982) *The Deindustrialization of America.* New York: Basic Books.

Mansfield, Edward (1968) *Industrial Research and Technological Innovation.* New York: Norton Press.

Mueller, Willard (1970) *Monopoly and Competition.* New York: Random House.

Saxenian, AnnaLee (1981) *Silicon chips and spatial structure. The industrial basis of urbanization in Santa Clara County, California.* University of California, Berkeley, Institute of Urban and Regional Development, Working Paper 345.

Scherer, Frederick (1980) *Industrial Market Structure and Economic Performance.* Chicago: Rand-McNally.

Teitz, Michael B., Glasmeier, Amy and Svensson, Douglas (1981) *Small business and employment growth in California.* University of California, Berkeley, Institute of Urban and Regional Development, Working Paper 348.

Walker, Hugh D. (1971) *Market Power and Price Levels in the Ethical Drug Industry.* Bloomington, IN: Indiana University Press.

Weiss, Marc (1984) Some public policy issues concerning employment strategy and high-technology industries, in Markusen, Ann and Weiss, Marc (eds.) *High Technology and the Future of Employment.* Berkeley, CA: Institute of Urban and Regional Development, University of California, Berkeley.

4

The American computer software industry: economic development prospects

PETER HALL, ANN R. MARKUSEN, RICHARD OSBORN and BARBARA WACHSMAN

*What is the future of the software industry
in the United States, and how will its structure
change over the next decade? Will it be a major
source of employment, and what will be the spatial
distribution of software firms and jobs?*

Of all the high-technology industries that have recently commanded national attention, the software industry is among the most promising. From less than $1 billion in the late 1970s, the industry's sales are expected to exceed $20 billion by 1990. Indeed, software will soon surpass the computer hardware industry in sales. Between 4000 and 4500 software firms now market over 10,000 products, and the average firm's sales are growing at a rate of more than 20 per cent per year. This sector is highly labour-intensive, offering the prospect of substantial job creation.

By reviewing the literature and conducting extensive interviews with California firms, we investigated four key issues for the economic development future of the software industry. First, what are the future growth prospects in this sector? Second, how innovative and competitive is this industry? Third, what are the future labour needs of this sector? Fourth, can any one region expect to retain and expand its software sector in the face of competition from other regions?

Growth Prospects in Software

Software can be defined in the broadest sense to include programs or instructions that modify or run computer hardware and extend its function beyond actual computing. The software industry encompasses products such as languages, programming tools, control programs, interpreters, monitors and supervisory systems, and professional and processing services.

Software is now the pacing factor in the further growth of computer use. But software remains a labour-intensive and costly progress. The rate of its improvement in cost performance during the past twenty-five years has been very low, much less than for hardware.

Of the estimated 4000 to 4500 independent software vendors, a large number are medium-sized, with some 2700 recording sales of less than $1 million in 1979 (Fishman, 1982, p. 268). In addition, there may be as many as 10,000 'mom-and-pop' programmers – professional consultants – in the Bay Area alone. Computer services revenues grew from an estimated $14.8 billion in 1980, with an overall growth rate of 24 per cent (with individual niches growing faster than 40 per cent), to over $22.1 billion in 1981. Analysts predict that the market will grow by 140 per cent by 1986 to $53 billion yearly. The annual cost of software in the United States is now approximately 2 per cent of gross national product and is expected to grow to 8.5 per cent of GNP by 1985 (Boehm, 1981, p. 17).

Table 1 Revenue growth by market segment.

Revenues	1980		1985		Average annual
	$ (billions)	%	$ (billions)	%	growth rates
Software products	2.6	12.4	8.4	24.9	42%
Professional services	3.4	23.5	7.5	21.4	27%
Processing services	8.8	59.1	18.8	53.7	17%

Source: ADAPSO, Sixteenth Annual Survey of the Computer Services Industry, July 1981.

The growth prospects for individual market segments are quite different and have serious implications for economic development planning. Software services fall into three broad categories: processing services; professional services; and software products. The current market shares of these three segments, and their expected growth rates, are shown in table 1. The smallest segment, software products, is expected to grow fastest in the early 1980s while the largest segment, processing services, will grow least rapidly. By 1985, the products group will have doubled its share and control 25 per cent of the market. Its superior performance will transform the software industry into a commodity rather than service producing sector. Production firms will not be tied into local markets and will thus tend to be more spatially concentrated. And, as we shall see below, they will not require as much manpower.

Competition and Continued Innovation

Competition in an industry can be measured by concentration ratios, which express the percentage of sales accounted for by the leading four, eight, twenty and fifty firms. Concentration in the software sector is somewhat influenced by concentration in the hardware sector. Large hardware manufacturers are also five of the top major suppliers of software services (for example IBM and Control Data). But even including these giants of software production, no single company commands more than 5 per cent of market share in any area, and the market remains extremely fragmented. This is distinctly unlike the hardware industry; the software market is not dominated by a single

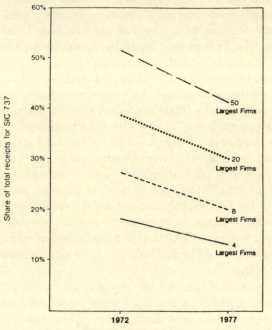

Figure 4.1 Concentration in SIC 737 largest firms' share of total US receipts, 1972–1977 (Source: Census of Service Industries)

giant competitor, as hardware is by IBM. Figure 4.1 clearly demonstrates that in the 1970s the software industry remained fragmented, becoming less concentrated over the period.

The 'typical' software company averages thirty to forty employees, with annual revenues of between $1 and $3 million. Annual growth is an average 20 per cent, with profits before taxes at 11 per cent, and average revenue per employee of $54,000 (*Dataguide*, 1981, p. II–4).

Entry into the market place is relatively easy for the independent computer services provider because little front-end investment is required. One person with one good idea can bring his-her idea to the marketplace and can easily carve a niche with a good product. As much as 80 per cent of software goods and services comes from small independents.

While these measures suggest considerable competition, it is also true that big multi-plant firms are gaining in share of sales. The share of all computer services receipts accounted for by single-unit firms was both substantial and rising during the 1970s, while the portion received by multi-unit firms with ten or fewer establishments dropped. The portion controlled by very large multi-unit firms was high and also rose between 1972 and 1977. The industry could be bifurcating into one of very large and very small firms, which could result in an innovation-slowing dominance by the giants.

Effective competition, of course, can emerge from firms outside the United States. The impact that Japanese competition has had in key areas of the computer hardware industry raises the question of whether software could be similarly affected. We asked our interviewees to assess the competition expected from Japan in their particular product areas. Half recorded that Japanese competition would not be significant. They cited impediments in Japanese business practices and culture (no venture capital, little entrepreneurial behaviour, excessive perfectionism, etc.); the fact that much software is specific to US culture (for example accounting packages); the 'culture gap'; and 'language barriers'. Those who believed that the Japanese will be significant competitors, especially in operating systems, noted that Japanese investment in software R&D is substantial and that the Japanese have the lead in education and training. The Japanese were also described as being more user-oriented in software design and pricing.

Competition is also affected by buyouts and vertical integration. Merger activity to achieve vertical integration will increase. Major hardware companies are now moving to acquire successful software houses in order to add value to their hardware and to satisfy consumer demand for complete computing packages. Data available on acquisition activity show that from January to June 1981, fifty-seven acquisitions occurred valued at $244 million, an increase of more than 50 per cent from the year before. Successful companies of the future will graduate from free-wheeling, engineering-oriented, entrepreneurial ventures to established firms run by Business-School-educated marketing and financial strategists. In many markets, there may be a transformation from multiple small, independent companies to a consolidated industry of a few conglomerates. But in some niches, there will still be lively activity among independents and large numbers of individual entrants.

In our view, the key to continued innovation is the maintenance of these small, competitive firms. New firms, often spun off from more established firms, help keep industry leaders on their toes and heighten the innovative spirit. Yet while the number of firms entering the industry is on the rise, the percentages of output and employment accounted for by large multi-establishment firms are increasing. Our interviews suggest that such growing concentration is not a function of production costs or economies, but is induced by several problems faced by the small innovative firm.

First, the present copyright laws offer firms little protection for new products. Software is treated as written materials, not a commodity, so that the more lenient copyright laws apply, rather than patent restrictions. Small firms face stiff legal costs if they pursue litigation. Many feel compelled to expand forward into sales and distribution to recoup their investment; some are driven to join a larger firm with a legal department and its in-place distribution system.

Second, firms in the initial stages of development face great difficulties raising capital. Our sample was drawn almost entirely from more mature firms that had surmounted these early development costs, yet access to investment funds clearly remains a problem for many would-be innovators. A firm at the start-up point has no assets to speak of, merely a team of eager and innovative personnel, which is not usable collateral for a bank loan. Even when programs exist in written form, banks refuse to consider them assets, again precluding access to bank funds. Capital needs at the beginning tend to drive small firms into mergers with larger firms that have internal funds at their disposal.

Third, formidable marketing problems confront small firms. A good product is not a money-maker unless it reaches its market. Most small firms have neither the expertise nor the resources to reach their targets. Many are thus driven toward merging with other companies who possess good distribution links and have access to broader geographical areas. Large firms, too, are driven by the desire to offer a full spectrum of products, encouraging buyouts of smaller and more youthful firms.

One important countervailing force favouring the small, innovative firm was detected in our study. Programmers as a group are a highly motivated, entrepreneurially minded group. Many have been drawn to the occupation precisely because of the chance to work in small groups and to have substantial control over their hours, product, and work environment. Despite attempts by many firms to enhance worker satisfaction through profit sharing and perquisites, turnover is high. High turnover is especially damaging to a software producer, and turnover rates appear to be greatest in larger firms and in those with more of a factory-like environment.

Occupational Structure, Labour Force Needs and Job Creation

Software production requires a large number of managerial, professional, and technical workers than most industries. For example, in national averages, the computer services sector (SIC 737) has a smaller portion of non-supervisory workers than the service industries as a whole. A detailed breakdown of the occupational distribution of the computer services sector in California is given in figure 4.2. On average, about half of the employees in this sector work directly with computers. Compared to manufacturing, the computer services sector in California has a very high portion of employees in management, professional, and technical occupations: 51 per cent compared to 19 per cent. The real 'production' workers in computer services are those in the clerical workers category. Thus about a third of employment growth in computer services is in well-paid skilled occupations with a relatively secure future, while the other two-thirds are relatively low-paid, less-skilled and less secure.

In the short run, labour shortages in the programming slots are critical. The president of Intel has predicted that unless radical new productivity tools are developed, over one million software engineers will be required over the next decade to service the micro market alone (*Electronics*, 1980 p. 43). Experts have estimated that programmer demand outstripped supply in 1980 by at least 50,000. As a result,

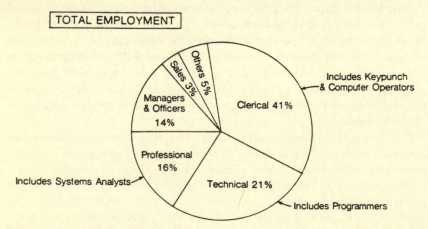

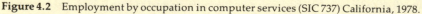

Figure 4.2   Employment by occupation in computer services (SIC 737) California, 1978.

competing firms offer programmers highly attractive salaries and benefits. At the same time, changes in product, job structure, and labour markets are helping to close the labour gap. For instance, 'software paraprofessionals' are being trained in an attempt to break down the development process by using lower-paid, less-skilled technicians to do routine work.

While immediate demand for university-trained computer scientists to design software is clear, other job training and educational implications are not. What other levels and/or fields of education are desirable for software designer jobs? What are the employment opportunities for minorities and women? Is the software industry the answer to plant closings in other industries? What kind of education will prepare people for the software design jobs of 1990 and 2001? From our interviews, we arrived at tentative answers to these questions.

Though there may be a fairly specific set of aptitudes required to design good software, there is quite a bit of variety, at present, in the educational background that programmers have and the kind of work they do. Most interviews indicated that the greatest need is for 'supertechs': systems programmers and architects, most of whom have Master's degrees or PhDs in computer science or electrical engineering. For the less-than-supertech level, aptitude plus experience were acceptable substitutes for academic degrees in computer science. In one firm 40 per cent of the programmers had no Bachelor's degree. A large percentage of the programmers for the State of California have less than four years of college. In most firms there are several 'self-made' types – including some legendary programmers who have backgrounds as musicians, PhDs in French history, and so forth.

In many firms, all or nearly all programmers are white males. Thus while popular impressions of programming cast it as a mixed gender occupation, our findings suggest that in the more creative software design profession (as distinct from routine programming in large institutions), men predominate. But we did notice a tendency for the incidence of women as programmers in a firm to be related to the presence of women in top management in that firm. This constitutes a strong argument for maintaining diversity among firms in the software industry and for encouraging affirmative-action programmes in business and education.

By any of a variety of measures present-day employment growth in computer/information industries in general, and in the software sector in particular, is colossal. One of our sources noted that if current growth rates continue, 20 per cent of the US labour force will be programmers by the year 2001. Figure 4.3 shows the projected job

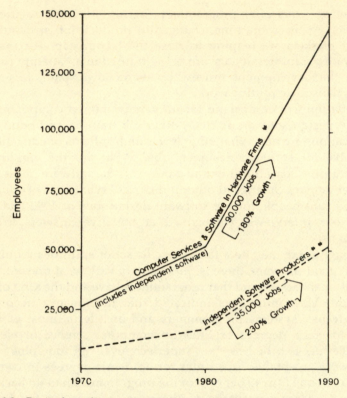

Figure 4.3 Revised employment projections for California: computer services and software in hardware firms, independent software producers, 1970–1990.

growth for California alone. But do estimates like this give a real basis for hoping that software growth could keep unemployment down? Our interviews gave us several reasons to be cautious about such assertions.

Present-day programmers are basically a professional class with a fairly specialized set of aptitudes and even specialized education. That implies that only a small portion of the people who can no longer expect to be employed in declining industries such as manufacturing could be redirected to software production as it is now structured. But there is a modest employment demand that can be filled by 'paraprofessionals' who have less than four years' college, provided that they have the special aptitudes required for programming. Furthermore, demand for non-programming personnel in software firms should not be overlooked. In firms for which we have estimates, 30–80 per cent of employees had non-programming jobs.

Optimistic estimates of future job growth must be tempered by long-range considerations. Information processing is a *derived demand*.

Hence it seems reasonable to expect that there will be upper limits on the place that computer industries will occupy in an economy. In even the most complex, and hence the most computerizable, industrial economies, the information-processing industries could level off at 4–5 per cent of the GNP or less. At present, demand for programmers and other software designers is far in excess of supply. As a result, software costs are dominated by high personnel costs. While computer hardware costs are dropping sharply, software development costs have been rising. The shortage of programmers places noticeable limits on the growth of the software industry, which, in turn, imposes limits on the growth of hardware sales.

All of this adds up to a strong drive to make programming more efficient, that is, to reduce the number of people required to produce the same number of units of software and/or to transfer as much work as possible from highly-trained (expensive) to lesser-trained (cheap) personnel. One model for this is the 'software factory', a hierarchical, assembly-line system in which software production is broken down into small stepwise tasks which are performed by less-skilled programmers passing their little pieces from cubicle to cubicle.

More likely is the development of *code generators*. Code generators will eliminate the need to master languages such as Pascal, PL/1 and even SpeakEasy, as communications with the computer come to resemble conversational English. Code generators will require more hardware, but as hardware becomes cheaper and programmers become more expensive, the familiar process of substituting machinery for labour will occur. Future computer systems may be designed so that more programming will be structured by end users who are not computer specialists.

This trend should have two effects on software employment in the next five to twenty years. First, demand for less-than-supertech programmers will level off. Second, the tasks and skills expected of programmers will fundamentally change. 'Programming' in future computer systems could involve four categories of employees:

1 The supertech, who designs and maintains nearly self-sufficient hardware/software systems.
2 The end user, whose main job is to do something else besides work with computers.
3 Professional intermediaries, who specialize in using computers in problem solving.
4 Paraprofessionals, who do lesser-skilled programming tasks.

Employment demand for supertechs is sure to be high, and they will probably be required to have considerable specialized computer education. The employment and education demands for the end-user category will depend on the rest of the economy.

In sum, there are reasons to be cautious about future employment demand. Present-day programmers come for the most part from a small, well-educated, professional segment of society with rather specialized aptitudes; programming will not provide many opportunities for those who have lost jobs in other sectors. And the very shortage of programmers and their resulting privileged status is giving strong impetus to the development of programming tools that could de-skill programmers or reduce the demand for them substantially.

What should be stressed in this scenario is the absence of an army of paraprofessional programmers, the retrained auto worker for example, projected in some accounts of high-tech labour demand. In their place will be a bifurcated labour market, with highly skilled PhDs employed in small numbers and a large group of user-employed computer specialists whose job responsibilities and pay levels might be akin to those in the clerical workforce today. This scenario has clear implications for the education of future software workers. Rather than retailoring our educational institutions, particularly universities, to meet an immediate demand for programmers with extensive computer language skills, we should be strengthening our basic education programmes, especially English, writing, mathematical, and logical skills.

The Spatial Distribution of Software Activity

Some insight into the spatial orientation and stability of software jobs could be gleaned from the Census and our California interviews. California is a microcosm of the nation, since it has a major share of the nation's software employment and is large enough to yield clear pictures of the urban bias of software firms.

California, with 10 per cent of the US population, accounts for approximately 16 per cent of overall computer service jobs. Its share of jobs in independent software firms is even higher – 20 per cent – and has been growing in recent years (see figure 4.4). On the other hand, its share of sales in the more routinized data-processing subsector fell in the 1970s. As data processing has become more like factory work and long distance communication cheap, other areas of the country with lower costs for land, buildings, and semi-skilled labour have become increasingly attractive. These trends suggest that a state like California may hold its edge in the more innovative, products development subsector while losing out in the standardized operations.

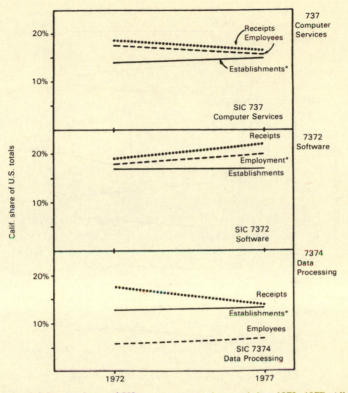

Figure 4.4 California share of US computer services activity, 1972–1977. All figures marked * are for establishment with payroll. (Source: Census of Service Industries)

This inter-regional pattern is mirrored by similar trends within the state across metropolitan and smaller city locations. Innovative operations remain in the largest metro centres, while data processing has decentralized. The attraction of other parts of the state seems to have affected the Los Angeles area most strongly. As figure 4.5 shows, the four-county Los Angeles area's share of California employment in data processing fell off after 1979. It also levelled off for the nine-county San Francisco Bay Area. In general there has been, and is still, more software activity in the Los Angeles basin (about 50 per cent of state totals) than in the San Francisco Bay Area (about 35 per cent of state totals), but the Bay Area is gaining in importance. These two metropolitan areas together are the sites for approximately 83 per cent of all software activity in the state.

Measured by employment, the two largest urban centres of the state taken together are losing their share of data processing but gaining slightly in independent software production. Again, this suggests that data-processing activities are going to cheaper locations, whereas

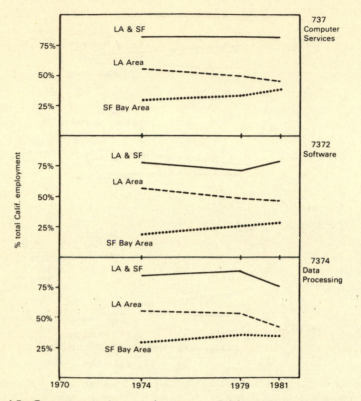

Figure 4.5 Computer services employment in California: Los Angeles area, San Francisco area employment; SIC 737, 7372, 7374, 1974–1981. (Sources: County Business Patterns; State of California Employment Development Department)

software design activities are remaining or concentrating in the urban areas. Software design firms may be showing a preference for urban areas where their skilled employees prefer to live and/or where there is a 'creative atmosphere' including the presence of major universities. Another factor may be that geographic proximity to large numbers of users is required for firms that must deal directly with their clients while designing or revising their software products and services.

Our interviews confirmed the general pattern believed to characterize all high-tech, innovative industries: firms are most likely to cluster together in a few locations. These spots generally have a top-rate university nearby, a substantial technical/professional labour force, good access to national communications and transportation systems, and urban/environmental amenities likely to draw and hold a professional labour force. However, certain features of software industry structure counteract this tendency.

First we detected a decentralizing force in the recent emphasis on marketing and servicing activities. Currently, a firm's need to reach national markets and to educate and consult with users often results in dispersal of new jobs to regional centres nearer to users.

A second decentralizing force is the concentration of a client in a particular region. Software firms serving the airlines, for instance, have followed airline company headquarters to Texas. The migration of software in search of centralized clients is most common on the service side of the industry and not as characteristic of software products. Again, the shift toward software products will tend to reinforce initial locational advantages, if the industry remains innovative in these centres.

A third force for decentralization is the widening differential between cost of living in high-tech metropolitan areas and other locations. Particularly problematic is the high cost of housing for professionals in those locations where software activity is clustered. Our informants echoed the concerns of the semiconductor and computer industry on this score, especially with respect to Silicon Valley. Yet other responses in our interviews suggested that professionals were quite willing to pay a premium to live in California, and particularly in urban areas, both because of nearby job alternatives and because of the general cultural and recreational advantages of the region. We believe that most firms are constrained by their employees' desire to remain in the Los Angeles area or the San Francisco Bay Area, despite the attraction of lower living costs at alternative sites.

On the other hand, changes in telecommunications will reinforce the pull of original centres. The continued improvement in telecommunications technology detaches software producers from clients spatially. Firms informed us that they expected to rely more and more on phone diagnosis of software problems rather than face-to-face service visits. This can be done as cheaply by long-distance telephone as by an intra-regional call. The net effect is to reinforce large-city communications centres. We originally expected that the same communications technology would detach programmers physically from software firms, but we encountered great scepticism in this regard from our interviewees. Most believe that programmers will be required to show up in the central office several times a week, to ensure communication and work progress.

One additional centre-reinforcing factor emerged from our interviews. Young software firms are concerned about their 'address'. They want to be identified with the heart of software inventiveness. For this reason, they prefer a Palo Alto or San Francisco address. For the same reason, unfortunately, most would shun the older city areas like Oakland, precisely those sites where unemployment is highest and jobs most in demand. Only for software firms involved in large-scale data processing, such as software for the insurance industry, are sites in places like Emeryville and Oakland attractive, because rents and secretarial costs are lower. It is our conclusion that existing centres, for all these reasons, possess continuing locational advantages.

Priorities for Economic Development Planning

Three different perspectives on government policy are possible. The first comes closest to the view of the industry itself. Firms currently populating the industry are concerned above all with the availability of well-educated programming talent. In addition, they favour tightening copyright laws, increasing basic university research, lowering the cost of living for their employees, and amplifying the financial resources available to growing firms.

A second perspective views the strength and job-creation potential of the industry as important state economic development goals, but takes a longer-run view of the industry's future, which may differ from the immediate expressed concerns of today's competitors. We believe that there are two issues that distinguish this posture from the previous one. First, the spectre of tremendous unmet demand for programmers contradicts our informants' views of future work structure in the industry. The programmer as we know him/her today may be relatively unimportant in the occupational structure of the future. Therefore, this perspective cautions against retooling education institutions to increase rapidly the supply of programmers.

Second, our sample of successful firms tended to dismiss the need for state intervention either into the capital market or into the marketing process. Many believed that government should leave the industry alone. Yet other, smaller and less successful firms may be unable to compete, and wistful would-be entrepreneurs unable to set up shop, because they confront the front-end capital problem or cannot break into an established distribution network. A healthy, competitive, innovative industry may require some form of governmental support for start-up capital and for joint marketing arrangements that would counteract the tendency towards concentration that we have documented.

A final perspective places the software industry's promise and problems in the context of the larger economy. No industry should be treated as a policy target without considering the claims of other industries; the impact of that industry on others, and the general costs and benefits it will bring to the society at large. Several issues of this sort are attached to the software industry. First, the software industry is a key component in the rapid mechanization of many other industries. Robotization requires sophisticated programs to direct mechanical arms to do what human labour has done for hundreds of years. While mechanization may eliminate difficult and dangerous work, and increase labour productivity, it also displaces workers who often have a difficult time finding alternative employment. We have found that very few industrial workers are apt to secure jobs in a new sector like software. Therefore, it is worth asking whether accelerating the rate of software innovation might not exacerbate adjustment problems in other sectors.

A second issue from this perspective is the effect on workers within the industry. Time constraints precluded a set of interviews with software programmers. We believe that there are a number of issues concerning health and safety (eye strain, stress, etc.) and job satisfaction that are critical to workers in the industry. Research and policy efforts should address these concerns. It is possible, too, that policies that accelerate the development of user-friendly software will eliminate the programmer's role, deskilling or displacing him in the process. State policy should avoid repeating the mistakes of a century of agricultural research that was largely dedicated to increasing crop productivity through mechanization, hybrids and pesticides, without considering the impact on agricultural workers.

State poicy should also avoid enhancing business prospects for software firms at the expense of their customers. An example where this could occur concerns the copyright area. While innovative firms need protection of their investments, stringent copyright provisions can also lead to monopoly profits and higher prices, which could impede the contribution software makes to productivity in other sectors. Similarly, state policy should avoid responding to complaints about the high cost of housing and transportation for this group of relatively highly-paid professionals without also considering the more pressing housing and transportation needs of lower-income groups in the population.

The limits of our research focus do not permit us to pass judgement on the tradeoffs between supporting a high-tech sector such as software and other demands on the state budget. We believe that software will be a net job creator, at least for another decade, but we do not believe that it will be a panacea for industrial restructuring problems. The best way for the state to aid the industry is to strengthen its commitment to basic education and to employ selective policy tools to engender innovation and competition.

References

Association of Data Processing Service Organization (ADAPSO) (1982) *Sixteenth Annual Survey of the Computer Services Industry.*

Boehm, B. W. (1981) *Software Engineering Economics.* New Jersey: Prentice Hall.

Center for the Continuing Study of the California Economy (1982) *California's Technological Future: Emerging Economic Opportunities in the 1980s.* Report of the California Department of Economic and Business Development.

Dataguide (1981) Spring, p. II–4.

Electronics (1980) Computer technology shifts emphasis to software: a special report. 8 May.

Fishman, K. D. (1981) *The Computer Establishment.* New York: Harper and Row.

5

Biotechnology and local economic growth: The American pattern

MARSHALL M. A. FELDMAN

*What is biotechnology and what are
the characteristics of biotechnology firms?
What is the nature of employment in this area of
high-technology and what factors determine
location and growth of the industry?*

Biotechnology is being hailed as a revolutionary technology which might cure cancer, meet the world's food requirements, and reshape the structure of industry in the last decades of the twentieth century. Some estimates predict as much as $15 billion in sales of biotechnology products by the year 2000. In response, entrepreneurs, enterprising scientists, venture capitalists, and multinational corporations are rushing to get a piece of the action.

If this new 'industrial revolution' does come to pass, it will undoubtedly alter the face of the urban landscape. But it is exceptionally difficult to predict *how* biotechnology will affect urban development. This paper attempts to draw out some of the implications of biotechnology for urban development; but doing so is very difficult. Good data on the technology as an industrial process are hard to come by so, at the risk of over generalizing, one must 'tease out' broad patterns from scant data.

Therefore, this chapter draws heavily on the Biotechnology Industry Survey (BIS) commissioned by the California Commission on Industrial Innovation (CCII). A random sample of ten firms, constituting about one-fifth of all biotechnology firms within the state, was selected for intensive interviews on topics such as considerations in location decisions, capital formation, labour force characteristics, and views on public policies toward biotechnology.[1] The research discussed here relates to the production process, labour force characteristics, and spatial location.

Understanding the production process is central to any understanding of employment growth, industrial location, and urban development. The production process strongly influences employment patterns and industrial location. In turn, the latter two elements are important determinants of urban development. Yet the connections between production processes and urban development are poorly understood.

The central role of the production process in industrial location is stressed by a number of authors (Massey and Meegan, 1982; Storper and Walker, 1983). A production process is not a merely technical combination of people, machines and materials. Production processes are simultaneously social and technological structures which both internalize and influence the larger social relations of society as a whole.[2] Therefore, the emphasis here is not only on biotechnology itself, but also on the social relations that characterize it in industrial settings.

The Technology

Industrial application of biotechnology basically consists of two components: genetic engineering and fermentation. During the 1950s, scientists discovered the genetic 'code' by which deoxyribonucleic acid (DNA) governs the reproduction of cells in all living organisms. By the 1970s, scientists had learned how to alter the code by 'recombination': the cutting of a piece of DNA and splicing of another piece of DNA in with the original. The new recombinant DNA (rDNA) molecule can then be inserted into a host micro-organism which then reproduces itself. Recombination DNA technologies provide engineered DNA which can give a micro-organism specific qualities not ordinarily found in nature. The process of designing DNA with the desired characteristics is termed genetic engineering, while the process by which micro-organisms are reproduced is called fermentation.

According to the Office of Technology Assessment, about 200 companies in the United States and over 500 worldwide use fermentation technologies (OTA, 1981, p. 50). The primary products of fermentation are commodities such as food proteins, insulin, inteferon, and haemoglobin. But such proteins can also be catalysts; for example, enzymes can be used to convert sugar to ethanol. However, many of these compounds can be produced by other, chemical means. Fermentation, and hence biotechnology, will be used only if it is economically competitive and socially acceptable.

A major obstacle to the spread of biotechnology is 'scale-up'. Many organisms which can be successfully fermented in the laboratory produce unstable results in large-scale fermentation, losing the desired characteristics induced in the laboratory. This problem and others like it still have to be solved, and they are hindering commercial applications of biotechnology.

Labour Force Characteristics

Many policy-makers see biotechnology as a potential source of new jobs, but one cannot assume that such jobs are necessarily *good* jobs or that they are available to everyone. Therefore, this section examines the composition of biotechnology's current labour force, the jobs currently found in biotechnology, and likely future trends in biotechnology employment.

Management

Managers of high-technology firms often require both technical and general business expertise. In the relatively new biotechnology field the ability to obtain capital also plays an important role. The 'typical' biotechnology firm is founded by one or more high-level scientists, usually PhDs with research positions at major universities, plus one or more persons with business expertise and connections to financial sources. Perhaps the most well-known example is Genentech which was founded in 1976 by Herbert W. Boyer, a University of Califonia scientist partly responsible for inventing the DNA technique, and Robert A. Swanson, a venture capitalist from the firm of Kleiner, Perkins, Caufield and Byers. Currently, Genentech's board of directors also consists of Donald L. Murfin, President of Lubrizol Enterprises, and Thomas J. Perkins, a partner in Kleiner-Perkins.

The actual mix of scientists and business people in biotechnology management varies a good deal. Based on the responses from eight firms to the BIS, about 52 per cent of top biotechnology managers have scientific backgrounds. This ranges from 14 per cent of one firm's board of directors to 75 per cent of another's.

In high-technology industries top managers tend to have technical backgrounds. According to Kuhn (1981, p. 55):

> nascent computer firms are, seemingly without exception, headed by engineer – or scientist – entrepreneurs who combine technical training with an interest, and possibly also some background, in business.

In fact, it is quite common for engineers to move into management. Engineering education and career patterns are increasingly oriented towards management (Noble, 1977, pp. 310ff). Added to this are those engineering specialities, for example industrial engineering, whose substance might well be considered managerial.

But, with the possible exception of bioengineering, scientific personnel in biotechnology companies do not have engineering backgrounds. Biotechnology scientists are trained in the 'pure sciences' of biology, chemistry, etc. Thus they do not have the same applied, business-oriented, training that the typical engineering graduate has. Firms headed by biotechnology scientists require more business expertise in the form of partners, co-directors, etc., with business backgrounds. While biotechnology firms may initially have a high proportion, even a majority, of research scientists among their top management, the most successful firms will increasingly have more traditional business people at the top. As biotechnology firms grow, the scientific founders are likely to be bought-out, confined to providing scientific advice and overseeing research, and/or serve as figureheads adding the prestige of their scientific reputations to the company's name.

Research and Development Jobs

Biotechnology researchers are granted a great deal of autonomy on the job. In part, this is because of the nature of scientific research, and in part this is used as a device to attract scientific talent. Because of this autonomy, biotechnology research practices vary widely, and it is difficult to come up with a single characterization of the R&D process. The stereotypical image of biological and chemical research conjures up an image of a white-coated scientist pouring chemicals from one flask to another. Alternatively, it pictures the same scientist checking on experimental test animals in their cages. Neither of these is the only image applicable.

One of the important developments in biotechnology R&D is the use of sophisticated computers for gene synthesis, process control, and mathematical modelling. Computerized gene synthesizers automatically control the introduction of reagents into DNA molecules to be cut (Alvarado-Urbino *et al.*, 1981). Computerized control is also used in the actual fermentation process (for both production and R&D purposes). Computers free the researcher for other work, much of which involves theorizing on the properties of specific chains of DNA and various chemical techniques of gene splicing. Hence, in addition to the image of the white-coated scientist, modern biotechnology R&D involves computer specialists, chemical engineers, electronics experts, and others qualified to maintain and utilize sophisticated, modern research equipment.

There are also a number of lower-ranking jobs. Biotechnology R&D requires bottle washers, caretakers for experimental animals, maintenance personnel, and other low-level employees, as well as the high-level scientific personnel. But because of the extremely varied conditions under which biotechnology research is undertaken, it is all but impossible to generalize about future task and job titles in R&D.

Biotechnology Production Occupations

Because of its newness and rapid growth, the small size of biotechnology firms, and the importance of secrecy, it is extremely difficult to obtain good data on occupations in biotechnology. Because the technology is so new, there are as yet no standardized job classifications. Furthermore, the diversity of firms within the industry means that there is as yet no 'typical' biotechnology firm. This is reflected in the variance of responses to the BIS: the percentage of all employees engaged in administration ranges from 9 per cent to 100 per cent (Feldman and O'Malley, 1982, p. 70). Hence, care must be taken in generalizing about jobs associated with the technology.

The largest occupational category in biotechnology is *professional and technical*, which is also the most visible and glamorous. Based on the responses to the BIS, this category comprises about 63 per cent of all employment in California biotechnology.

Actual jobs included in this category may involve PhD biologists, graduate chemistry students, computer programmers, engineers, and other diverse specialties. Some have considerable control over their own working conditions: setting their own pace of work, etc., while others work in closely supervised settings. The BIS indicates that about 12 per cent of total biotechnology employment fits the former description, while about 48 per cent fits the latter (Feldman and O'Malley, 1982, p. 71).

Whatever the true split between independent and closely supervised work, only a part of the independence granted these workers is due to specific technical requirements. Independence and flexibility are used by biotechnology firms as a means of attracting qualified personnel. It is therefore likely that any future 'loosening up' of the market for biotechnology professionals, coupled with any 'deskilling' of the research and development process, will translate into a somewhat more closely supervised and less independent professional workforce.

As employment in biotechnology increases, it is unlikely that professional and technical employment will keep pace. Presently, firms are primarily research outfits, and current professional and technical employment is therefore closer to the 'steady-state' level than is employment in other occupations. As production increases, there will be a disproportionate increase in other occupational categories, although such increases may not be in the firms currently employing high percentages of professional and technical workers (Kuhn, 1981, pp. 90–1).

The second most populous occupational category in biotechnology is *clerical*. Based on the BIS, approximately 53 per cent of administrative jobs are clerical and 47 per cent are managerial. Using these figures yields an estimate of 17 per cent of all California biotechnology workers in clerical jobs and 15 per cent in managerial jobs. This estimate is reasonable compared to similar figures for other high-technology industries.[3] Clerical work includes jobs that facilitate record keeping, reporting, and communications. It therefore seems reasonable that such administrative functions would expand roughly in proportion to total biotechnology employment.

The third most populous occupational category in biotechnology is *management*. Because they supervise sophisticated research activites, many biotechnology managers have advanced degrees in related fields. But, as biotechnology expands, there will also be a need for managers with expertise in non-technical areas such as personnel, sales and marketing, investment, and the other functions necessary for the running of a 'mature' corporation. Because of the independent nature of their work, professional and technical workers experience less supervision than do other workers. Therefore, as biotechnology employment grows, it is likely that the ratio of managers to all employees (currently about 3:20) will increase. Hence growth in managerial occupations should be more than proportionate to the growth in all biotechnology jobs.

Because there is virtually no biotechnology production as yet, very few persons are employed in *floor-level supervision or production*. Estimates based on the BIS give about 2 per cent of all biotechnology workers as production workers and less than 1 per cent as floor-level supervisors. But the ratio of floor-level supervisors to production workers is 2:5, considerably higher than the ratio of managers to professional and technical workers. As biotechnology production expands, it seems likely that this ratio will decrease, but it is difficult to say by how much. Undoubtedly, the long-run proportionate increase in both production workers and their supervisors will be the largest for any occupational category, as more and more biotechnology production comes on-line.

The nature of the work performed by production workers can vary a great deal, depending on the nature of the product, the production process, and the specific tasks within the overall division of labour of the firm. Given the nature of fermentation technology, the 'typical' biotechnology production worker will most likely be involved in tending vats. It is too early to say much more about what will be involved because many of the major technological innovations necessary to make biotechnology products competitive relate to 'scale-up'.

Neither can much be said about possible health and safety hazards to production workers. The fact that biotechnological manufacturing involves living organisms indicates that it should be relatively safe for other living things. Especially when replacing processes involving dangerous chemicals, high pressures, and high temperatures, biotechnology may result in important increases in worker safety. In fact, many expect the savings in expenditures for worker safety to be a major factor in making biotechnological processes economically competitive. But experience shows that the dangers of industrial processes are often not discovered until well after they are first put into use. Hence, while biotechnology appears to offer greater safety for production workers, only experience will tell.

Finally, there is a small proportion of biotechnology employment in *maintenance*. Based on BIS data, slightly over 2 per cent of all biotechnology employment is in maintenance. Undoubtedly, as biotechnology begins to be applied to actual production, this will grow. In fact, given the passive nature of fermentation technology, it is likely to be difficult to distinguish maintenance workers from production workers. The former maintain machinery and physical plant, but with fermentation technology much of the production work relates to maintaining machinery.

Productivity and Labour Force Growth

Good time-series data and forecasts of biotechnology employment are very difficult to come by. National employment in synthetic genetics is certainly below 10,000 and probably closer to 5000.[4] Table 5.1 shows time-series data for California synthetic genetic firms based on estimates from the BIS. As the table shows, 1981 employment was less than 0.02 per cent of all employment in the state.

But the growth of synthetic genetic employment has been dramatic. Since 1976, employment has increased more than ten-fold. The compounded annual rate exceeds 50 per cent, and if this rate were to continue, over 156,000 persons would be employed in synthetic genetics by 1990. Realistically, it is more accurate to assume employment increasing at a constant annual amount. Extrapolating past patterns yields a low estimate of about 6650 employees in 1990 (Feldman and O'Malley, 1982, pp. 75–6).

Because past trends do not include any period of actual production of commercial products, much better ballpark estimates can be obtained by comparing biotechnology with other fermentation-based industries. In the malt beverage industry (SIC 2082) 1977 output was 2617 barrels per production worker – a productivity increase of over 30 per cent since 1972! In medicinals and botanicals (SIC 2833) value added per wage dollar increased by over 50 per cent, while in pharmaceutical preparations it declined by just under 7 per cent during this same period. But value added per wage dollar is sensitive to relative prices and does not accurately reflect physical productivity, so the malt beverage industry is a better comparison for biotechnology productivity growth.[5]

Table 5.1 Employment growth in California biotechnology.

| Year | Total statewide civilian employment | | Biotechnology employment* | | |
	Employment (1000s)	Indexed (1976=100)	Employment	Indexed (1976=100)	Percentage of California employment
1976	8820	100	279	100	0.003
1978	9890	112	279	100	0.003
1979	10285	117	306	110	0.003
1980	10443	118	630	226	0.006
1981	10528	119	1855	665	0.018
1982	—	—	3064	1098	—

* Estimates based on BIS sample respondents and multiplied by 5.57 (=7/39) to provide population estimates. Statewide employment figures are not available for 1982.
Sources: California Statistical Abstract (1981), *California Economic Indicators* (November, 1981).

Productivity in biotechnology is undoubtedly going to be high. For example, it is estimated that 181 production workers could produce enough enzymes to meet total 1982 worldwide demand. Synthetic genetics will be heavily used as an alternate production technology for products currently manufactured by chemical means. So total *net* employment growth due to biotechnology will be a good deal lower than gross employment growth. Nonetheless, making a series of generous assumptions about employment growth it is estimated that national employment in synthetic genetics may be as much as 44,000 in 1992 (Feldman and O'Malley, 1982, pp. 77–80). This is smaller than the brewery industry today and reflects gross employment growth, not net.

Given the large size of markets involved – as much as $12 million by 1990 (OTA, 1981) – many firms are working on further automating fermentation technology. Therefore it is likely that productivity will increase at an even more rapid pace. On the other hand, firms already claim that no further automation is possible in the R&D process. In order to maintain and increase productivity in R&D, biotechnology firms utilize various forms of 'bureaucratic' control and incentives: employee ownership, bonuses, self-management, and recognition for publications, patents and royalties (Feldman and O'Malley, 1982, pp. 80–1).

Social Characteristics

Data on the social composition of the biotechnology labour force are quite poor (Feldman and O'Malley, 1982, p. 81–2). The BIS yields estimates of 41 per cent of California biotechnology workers as female and 21 per cent as minorities. The latter figure is undoubtedly inflated because many foreign nationals working as research scientists were included in the 'minority' category by respondents. The figure for female employees is roughly comparable with statewide figures, but women are extremely over-represented in traditionally female jobs: it is estimated that 94 per cent of clerical workers in biotechnology are female. On the other hand, women are only slightly under-represented in professional and managerial jobs: 37 per cent of managers and professionals are female. But because no data on women's decision-making powers or spans of authority are available, this figure cannot be used to infer that women are close to being equally represented in higher-ranking positions. By the same token, the fact that foreign nationals were classed as minorities and that firms do not keep data on occupational classifications by ethnicity preclude any comment about the position of minorities in biotechnology.

The Spatial Location of Biotechnology Firms

The Geographical Incidence of US Firms

There are approximately 113 synthetic genetic firms in the United States and at least another twenty-seven worldwide. The state with the most biotechnology employment is California, which has thirty-nine firms employing roughly 30 per cent of national biotechnology employment.[6]

Nationally, biotechnology is highly concentrated. Fifty per cent of all firms are located in California or Massachusetts, and 70 per cent are located in these two states plus Connecticut, New York, and Maryland (see table 5.2). Similarly, employment is concentrated but in a different set of states: California, 31 per cent; Colorado, 20 per cent; Maryland, 14 per cent; Kansas, 10 per cent; and Florida, 6 per cent. Massachusetts, the second-ranking state in number of firms, ranks sixth in number of jobs.

Table 5.2   Location of biotechnology firms by state and region.

Location	Firms		Employment		Annual revenues ($ million)	
	No.	%	No.	%	Amount	%
New England						
Connecticut	6	5	91	3	4.5	3
Massachusetts	18	16	175	5	3.0	2
Middle Atlantic						
Delaware	1	1	—	—	—	—
New Jersey	4	4	51	3	—	—
New York	12	11	110	3	1.8	1
Pennsylvania	2	2	35	1	0.2	0
South Atlantic						
Florida	3	3	185	6	3.89	2
Georgia	1	1	—	—	—	—
Maryland	5	4	470	14	11.6	7
Virginia	1	1	—	—	—	—
East North Central						
Illinois	2	2	—	—	—	—
Indiana	2	2	9200*	—	686.1*	—
Michigan	1	1	5	0	—	—
Wisconsin	1	1	15	—	0.5	0
West North Central						
Kansas	1	1	315	10	27.5	17
Minnesota	1	1	35	1	1	1
Nebraska	1	1	—	—	—	—
West South Central						
Lousiana	1	1	—	—	—	—
Texas	1	1	—	—	—	—
Mountain						
Colorado	4	4	656	20	85	52
Montana	1	1	5	0	—	—
Utah	1	1	85	2	2.6	2
Pacific						
California	39	34	1030	31	21.6	13
Washington	4	4	15	0	—	—
Total	113	100	3278	100	163.19	100

* This figure is for Miles Laboratory and excluded from the computations.
Source: F. Eberstadt & Co., Inc.

The pattern of revenues is even more concentrated. One state, Colorado, accounts for over 50 per cent of all revenues. Kansas is second (17 per cent) and California, third (13 per cent). Fully 80 per cent of all reported revenues are concentrated in three states! But revenues are a poor indicator of biotechnology activity because few firms are marketing products as yet. Furthermore, one Colorado firm, Argrigenetics, accounts for 650 out of 656 jobs and 100 per cent of the revenues reported there. Agrigenetics specializes in seeds and soil bacteria, synthetic genetics playing a partial role in its total activities.[7] Thus, one may conclude that synthetic genetic employment is concentrated in California and Massachusetts, with New York a close third. This pattern has been reported in the national press and is similar to that of other high-technology industries (for example computer manufacturing, see Kuhn, 1981, pp. 74ff).

The BIS and the above data indicate that biotechnology firms are *also* remarkably concentrated *within* states. Table 5.3 shows the spatial distribution of biotechnology firms within California.[8] The most striking feature of this table is the extremely high degree of concentration in the San Francisco-Oakland area. Almost half (twenty) of California's biotechnology firms are located in this area. Even more striking is the fact that over 91 per cent of the state's biotechnology employment is located in this area. San Diego is the major biotechnology centre in Southern California. Twenty per cent of all synthetic genetic firms are located in the San Diego area. In addition, most of the firms in Santa Ana are located in nearby Newport Beach. Other centres are located in areas adjacent to north of San Francisco-Oakland: Davis and San Rafael.

Table 5.3 Location of biotechnology firms within California.

Area	Firms		Employees	
	No.	%	No.	%
Los Angeles	0	0	0	0
Santa Monica	1	2		
Pasadena	1	2	12	1
Newbury Park	1	2	10	1
Alhambra	2	5		
San Diego	8	20	61	5
Santa Ana	2	5	—	—
Bakersfield	1	2	—	—
San Francisco	13	32	656	55
Oakland	7	18	430	36
San Rafael	1	2	—	—
Santa Clara	1	2	—	—
Davis	2	5	17	1
Total	40	100	1186	100

The Determinants of Biotechnology Location

Perhaps the most obvious determinant of location for biotechnology firms is proximity to major university research centres performing rDNA research. This accounts for the two locations with the most biotechnology firms: the San Francisco Bay Area and the Boston area. Many of the firms in these two areas located there because either the firms themselves were founded by former faculty members from nearby universities, or members of the firms' research staff desire to continue their academic activities by teaching and participating in seminars, etc. at nearby universities.

The BIS indicates that three locational factors are most important in attracting biotechnology firms: proximity to major research centres (for their research libraries, graduates, students, and academic staffs), the quality of residential life (in order to attract and retain high calibre researchers), and the potential for growth (space for physical expansion, transportation facilities, etc.). One problem mentioned frequently in the San Francisco Bay Area is the high cost of employee housing. Other problems mentioned in connection with San Francisco are distance from the other major population and academic centres in the nation (specifically, the northeast), poor ground access, land costs, lack of proximity to field sites, taxes, and red tape in state agencies.

In contrast, several factors commonly used to explain location are uniformly ranked as having 'minor importance' or being 'not important' on the BIS: proximity to markets, availability of low-cost labour, availability of reliable energy, government incentives, proximity to major suppliers, availability of utilities, and proximity to major competitors. Availability of business services, taxes, and highway transportation are of moderate importance. Air transportation is generally considered to be important, while rail and mass transit are of mixed importance.

Asked if they would consider moving, several firms replied that they either would consider moving or already had moved. These firms almost uniformly said they would (had) move(d) because they needed more space for expansion, but all of these firms said they would (had) move(d) within their present region. Three firms mentioned that they would consider opening facilities outside the area. In one case, the reason for doing so would be closer proximity to markets (once production of marketable products began). Another firm mentioned opening a branch in Europe in order to tap into new markets and networks of biotechnology researchers. The third response along these lines was a firm that said it would consider opening a facility outside the area in order to enter into a joint venture with another biotechnology firm.

In sum, the major positive factors influencing the location of biotechnology firms are proximity to major research centres, residential quality of life, and potential for expansion. The first of these restricts the general region in which firms locate, while the other two influence *where within the region* firms locate. In general, spatial considerations are very important in the decision to open new facilities. There is a certain attraction for locating new facilities *outside* the present region in order to tap into different networks of researchers and new markets.

Location and Local Growth Performance

In standard export-base theory, the local multiplier acts to increase local demand. In turn, this effect 'ripples through' the local economy, producing local growth. But care must be taken in applying these results to biotechnology. True, biotechnology is generally new growth. But the end result of much new biotechnology will be substitutes for already existing production processes and products. In fact, biotechnology may be less labour and capital intensive than competing technologies. Hence, the net effect may be a decrease in the rate of growth when compared to that of the competing technology.

Given a competitive private market economy, public policy cannot make decisions to substitute non-competitive technologies that result in higher rates of local growth, *ceteris paribus*. If local, or even national, government were to make such an attempt, local industry would be at a competitive disadvantage with competitors from outside the local area, state, or country.

On the other hand, biotechnology will also develop completely new products – that is, products that are not substitutes for presently existing ones. In such cases, biotechnology would generate new growth. The difficulty is in estimating the extent of such growth, especially on the local level.

As a rule, biotechnology firms do not purchase large proportions of non-labour inputs. A certain amount of new facility construction may be generated by biotechnology firms, but raw materials, supplies, and capital equipment purchases are not the major cost items in biotechnology R&D. Capital equipment, and to a lesser extent raw materials, are likely to be more important in biotechnologically-produced products once 'scaled-up' production comes on line. Given the current state of the industry, it is not at all clear that such facilities will be built near biotechnology R&D facilities. The location of production will depend on very different kinds of labour and raw materials costs than those borne by biotechnology R&D facilities. It is reasonable to expect some local spin-offs; pilot projects will probably be located near R&D facilities to facilitate monitoring of new processes. But once the production process is perfected, very different locational factors will come into play.

Also, the supplies purchased by biotechnology firms seem to be of two kinds: relatively inexpensive items commonly produced locally (for example, lab supplies) and more costly, specialized equipment purchased from national suppliers. In either case, most analysts predict that the total amounts involved will not be exceptionally large.

On the other hand, the market for biotechnology products will, in all likelihood, be very large. Industry analysts predict a total sales volume of roughly $3 billion by 1990 (Patterson, 1981, p. 66). These sales will be international in scope. Hence, the biotechnology industry is likely to bring a good deal of money through, if not into, local economies where biotechnology firms are located. The major economic impact of biotechnology may therefore be indirectly through the growth of the local tax base, rather than directly through local economic growth multipliers.

Notes

1 It may be that this sample is too small and localized for any broad generalizations. But California leads the nation in biotechnology employment, and the sample represents over 16 per cent of national biotechnology employment. For more information on the BIS, see Feldman and O'Malley (1982).
2 See Noble (1977) for discussions of the mutual interaction of technical and social relations of production. Even if production is conceptualized as simply a matter of technique, the choice of technique in a capitalist economy depends on the *social* division of the economy's net product.
3 For example, Kuhn (1981, p. 88) estimates that about one-fifth of all workers in computer manufacturing are clerical.
4 See Feldman and O'Malley (1982, pp. 74–80) for an extended discussion of the problems involved in making accurate estimates of biotechnology employment.
5 If anything, the figure of 30 per cent may be low. Potential profits in biotechnology are acting as an impetus for increasing the productivity of fermentation processes.
6 These figures for revenues and, to a lesser extent, employment are undoubtedly distorted because data of this sort on smaller firms are not available, but firms for whom these date are available, are diversified in fields other than biotechnology.
7 These figures are based on data from F. Eberstadt & Co updated with information from Dun & Bradstreet. A discussion of the problems with these data is given in Feldman and O'Malley (1982, pp. 18–19).
8 Table 5.3 should be interpreted with care. Employment figures are unavailable for most firms, and these are excluded from the computations, but included in the overall counts.

References

Alvarado-Urbino, G., *et al.* (1981) Automated synthesis of gene fragments. *Science*, **214** (4518), pp. 270–4.

Feldman, M. and O'Malley, E. (1982) *The Biotechnology Industry in California*. Sacramento: California Commission on Industrial Innovation.

Kuhn, S. (1981) *Computer Manufacturing in New England: Structure, Location and Labor in a Growth Industry*. Cambridge, Mass: Harvard MIT Joint Center for Urban Studies.

Massey, D. and Meegan, R. (1982) *The Anatomy of Job Loss: the How, Why and Where of Employment Decline*. London/New York: Methuen.

Noble, D. F. (1977) *America by Design*. Oxford/New York: Oxford University Press.

Office of Technology Assessment (OTA) (1981) *Impacts of Applied Genetics: Micro-organisms, Plants and Animals*. Washington DC: US Government Printing Office.

Patterson, W. P. (1981) The rush to put biotechnology to work. *Industry Week*, **210**, pp. 64–70.

Storper, M. and Walker, R. (1983) The theory of labor and the theory of location. *International Journal of Urban and Regional Science*, **7** (1), pp. 1–43.

6

High-technology industries and the future of employment

MARC A. WEISS

How should high-technology be defined?
What type of employment does it create and
what is its effect on other employment sectors?
What part can economic development policy
play in the overall employment process?

Discussions of deliberate government policy to subsidize and encourage the growth of high-technology industry confront three sets of problems: first, how to define high-technology industry; second, how to determine the goals and distributional impacts of an economic development programme; third, deciding upon the appropriate means for implementing such a programme.

What is a High-Technology Industry?

In previous policy debates, there has been a modest amount of disagreement and a great deal of confusion over just what precisely are the 'high-technology industries'. How does 'high technology' differ from 'low' and 'medium' technologies? Is the 'high technology' utilized in the production process or is it contained in the final product? Is it connected with manufacturing or distribution, goods or services? Must it be a relatively new invention or innovation, or can it be of less recent vintage?

'High-tech' definitions vary widely at the margin, but almost all include computers and microelectronic components (integrated circuits). While it is true that recent advances in information processing, combined with developments in electronic communications, are bringing dramatic changes to our everyday life, the reason why the above industries are singled out in a policy sense is primarily economic: they have been 'growing' while other parts of the economy have been stagnating. Growing in what way? In output and gross sales revenue, particularly as major export commodities. Thus, they have been important in helping alleviate the US balance of trade deficit. But the largest US export industry is agricultural products, which has also been growing quite rapidly in the past decade. Agriculture, however, is not considered to be high tech because while it uses considerable high technology in the production process, the export product itself is raw food. Oil and gas drilling equipment and aerospace and military equipment are also leading and growing US export items. These would seem to involve high technology in both production and product, yet they too are frequently excluded from lists of high-technology industry.

One reason why the latter two might be excluded is because their 1970–80 growth in employment has been small compared to the absolute and percentage employment growth in computers and electronic components. And yet recombinant DNA bioengineering is also included on many lists of high tech, even though it has brought no significant employment thus far, nor is it expected to bring much employment for quite some years. In fact, the biotech 'industry' is not an industry at all, but a technology that could potentially be used in a number of different production processes to produce a variety of products. Most of the production is likely to be done under the auspices of major pharmaceutical companies, which would seem to be pretty high tech in any case, and certainly have been growing in employment and exports. Yet, drugs are another industry generally left off most high-tech lists.

Despite the focus on manufactured goods, many high-tech lists include the computer software industry, which is a service. The reason for this inclusion is because the growth of software and 'hardware' in computers is so closely tied together and interdependent. But, medical services are also growing very fast in employment, and are highly interdependent with the rapidly accelerating manufacture of advanced technological medical equipment. Despite these similarities, the health industry is also generally not considered to be part of the high-tech category.

The methodological problems seem endless. One definition stands out as having logical consistency in measurement and application. This definition, which is being used increasingly in academic and policy studies, is that a high-technology industry (which may or may not have a US Department of Commerce Standard Industrial Classification) is defined by an above average percentage of its labour force engaged in engineering, scientific, professional, and technical work. For example, one grouping of high-technology industries for California averaged 25 per cent of the labour force in these categories, whereas the proportion in the total California workforce is 5 per cent.

Such a definition, while having the virtue of modest precision, also leads to policy problems, which I will discuss in the sections below.

Another definition, less measurable but perhaps more precise, is that the industries on the various lists for government policy purposes are chosen on the basis of political criteria. At the federal level, the key criteria seems to be that the high-tech industries are now manufacturing industries which have grown rapidly in economic power and importance in the past two decades, but have not as yet (with the exception of IBM) organized sufficiently to lobby for their special needs with Congress and federal agencies. This, more than anything else, is what distinguishes them from older and well-organized industries like oil and gas, aerospace, medical, pharmaceutical, etc. At the state and local level, the fact that information technology production has been a source of growth in substantial numbers of small businesses and also in significant expansion of branch plants by fast-growing corporations in the past decade means that states and localities are now discussing the adoption of policies specifically to attract new small firms or branch plants or larger firms in these particular industries. Whatever relatively new industry these governments hope to attract automatically becomes high tech. Newer fields with no record of significant employment growth also get included on various lists in the hope that a state or locality can duplicate an 'agglomeration' strategy similar to that in Silicon Valley in California or Route 128 in Massachusetts. Thus, the newer the technology (robotics, photovoltaics, bioengineering), the more potential for 'getting in on the ground floor'. In its most fundamental sense, then, high-technology industry generally means new technology goods-producing industries (and related services) which are still a long way from market saturation and over-production, or if they are beginning to face the problem of global competition, are now organizing to make demands for government assistance to preserve the gains in market share of the previous decade.

Employment the Key: How Much, What Type, Who Gets, and Where?

Despite the disparity in definitional criteria, clearly the most important single element from the standpoint of public policy goals is employment. All the high-tech industries on any list are there either for their actual record of rapid job growth in recent years or for their presumed long-run potential for significant job growth. The problem is that even assuming fantastic growth levels, these industries cannot possibly absorb all the surplus labour from other sectors nor accommodate all the new entries into the labour force each year. If every level of government everywhere pursues high-tech development strategies, most of them will surely be doomed to failure. In California, which is a national leader in high-tech employment (20 per cent of the US total according to one study), these industries still employ less than 5 per cent of the total state workforce. The business services sector is nearly as large, and the medical services sector employs more people than high technology (Center for the Continuing Study of the California Economy, 1982).

New technology producers go through product and profit cycles just like any other industry or sector, and some areas of electronics production are already facing world overcapacity with employment stagnating or even declining. Further, in addition to layoffs and cutbacks due to competition and excess capacity, many firms which are still experiencing growth in output and sales are reducing the size of their labour force due to automation.

Cutbacks in employment due to competition and automation mean that strategies of pursuing and subsidizing high-tech firms on the basis of past performance in employment growth and/or future potential for expansion of output may be self-defeating, unless the people in the jurisdiction will benefit from other employment linkages, derived demand employment effects, or from taxing the gross revenues and net income related to future expansion. For example, Feldman and O'Malley (1982) estimate that, at best, gene-splicing in California will employ only 14,000 people by 1990, or 0.01 per cent of the state's total labour force at the time. However, there may be substantial indirect positive employment impacts, and state and local governments might be able to tax the revenues accruing to these highly capital-intensive gene-splicing firms, either or both of which would help justify a public policy of support for the infant industry, despite its very modest short-term potential for direct job creation.

Direct vs. Indirect Jobs: Net Gain or Net Loss?

The issue of direct versus indirect job creation is crucial with relation to the growth and development of high-technology industries. The case of small direct job growth but large indirect job growth (which is hypothetical in the case of bioengineering) is very untypical. The much more common case is that of modest to substantial direct job growth, but massive indirect job loss. The production of new information-processing, communication, and other technologies is leading to a virtual revolution in the organization of work and society.

Such changes involve a vast retooling and restructuring of all forms of employment (as well as consumption) in terms of both geographic location/organization and social division of labour. *Business Week* (1981) predicts that 25 million current jobs will be eliminated in the next two decades due to the introduction of new technologies. Government policies that encourage the faster development, production, and utilization of new technologies in order to promote direct job creation in specific high-tech industries may be losing sight of the larger picture. The net job loss, the disruption to workers' lives and livelihoods and to the well being of communities may be devastating. Government economic strategies for private sector job creation that involve commitment of public resources through various subsidy programmes must take into account the total employment and community welfare impacts of an 'economic development' policy. While major technological changes can have beneficial long-term productivity and income effects, depending on the structure of ownership and control and the distribution of wealth and income, public policy planning for employment must be designed to enhance the continuity and stability of job opportunities and standards of living, so as not to accelerate the pace of social disruption and lost human potential brought about by job displacement, high unemployment, community disinvestment, and income loss. In other words, a high-tech employment strategy can only be considered as part of a much broader set of overall policies for job preservation and creation. Without such larger considerations, high-tech policy may be wasteful, misguided, and even counterproductive.

The Dual Labour Force and the Vanishing Middle

As mentioned above, one prominent characteristic of high-tech sectors is the substantial proportion of the labour force in the scientific, professional and technical category. These are jobs which generally require at least an undergraduate college degree, and very often advanced graduate training. They are well-paid jobs with relatively decent working conditions and they are overwhelmingly filled at present by white males less than forty-five years old.

Another characteristic of the high-tech labour force is that a substantial proportion consists of low-paid assembly and clerical work. In addition to poor pay and benefits, these jobs often do not provide very satisfactory working conditions, particularly in the unskilled assembly work. Those hired to perform such jobs are overwhelmingly female and very large percentage from ethnic minorities.

Most high-tech firms are also distinguished by being entirely non-union, that is, none of their workers are organized and represented by trade unions for the purpose of collective bargaining with the owners and managers. Certainly the lack of any union organization and representation is one reason why clerical and assembly workers' wages and working conditions have not significantly improved during a decade of high profits and rapid expansion in these industries. The lack of unions for professional and technical workers is more problematic, though it might be argued that high-tech managers' fear of unionization (as well as of employee turnover) by their white-collar workforce has led to more beneficial conditions of employment than might otherwise be the case. It could also be argued that a major reason for innovative labour policies at the high end of the employment scale has to do with a demand-supply imbalance in favour of workers with certain technical skills, which may be one reason why many employers are insisting that universities should vastly increase the supply of engineers and scientists, whereas the various engineering and scientific associations are less enthusiastic about such an undertaking.

Since the growth of direct high-tech employment is often pointed to as a possible solution for the problems of employment decline and plant closings in other sectors of US manufacturing industry, we can readily see that the structure of the high-tech labour force poses major difficulties for solving the employment problems of 'blue-collar' decline. Since the highest single proportion and fastest-growing segment of high-tech jobs is in the scientific, professional, and technical categories, skilled manufacturing workers displaced from other industries are, at present, totally unqualified for the bulk of these professional and technical jobs. In most cases, a displaced manufacturing worker would have to undergo anywhere from two to ten years of education and training to be qualified for these positions, during which time he or she could not possibly be earning more than a fraction of his or her previous full-time pay and benefits.

While former crafts or factory workers might be qualified to perform clerical or assembly work in high-tech industries with only one year or less of education and training (or perhaps none at all), they would probably be facing a 50–80 per cent pay cut, plus a loss of a great deal of control over the work environment that they had previously attained through trade union organization. However, even in cases where displaced workers do apply for high-tech jobs that do not require significant college-level education and training, they generally are not hired by high-tech employers because many employers feel these workers are more likely to express dissatisfaction with their wages and working conditions and be more likely to support efforts to organize their workers into trade unions (Bluestone and Harrison, 1982).

Not only is an important segment of the 'middle' of the US job structure vanishing, in the sense of relatively well-paid, stable, skilled manufacturing-related employment, but the new types of low-paid high-tech assembly work that have grown so rapidly in the past decade are also beginning to disappear. Some of this work has been shifted overseas to countries where average wage levels are significantly lower, corporate and governmental discipline more repressive, and unions virtually non-existent. In addition, many of the large numbers of assembly jobs that still remain in the United States will be automated out of existence within the next two decades. Clerical jobs will still grow, but perhaps at a less rapid rate, as certain categories of clerical employment are also being automated through the new technologies of the 'electronic office'.

Where jobs in high tech are not being eliminated outright, in many instances a process of 'deskilling' is taking place where previously growing professional, technical, and clerical fields become more capital-intensive, less skilled, and much lower paid. This process is taking place not only within high tech, but throughout the productive economy as a result of the development and introduction of new technologies into production (and service) processes. Even in such a seemingly labour-intensive field as the writing of computer software, a great deal of automation and deskilling is taking place which will eliminate many of the now attractive jobs at the less-than-PhD-degree level. Further, the process of creating such a wide gap between the two main categories of employment (top professionals versus un-skilled labour) means that the notion of a career ladder, which has traditionally been very important in terms of skill and pay upgrading within the labour force, may also be disappearing as a consequence of advancing high tech. For policy purposes, the question of what kind of jobs and career opportunities is as important as the simple raw numbers of projected available employment.

Another issue in addition to job and income quality is the question of who gets the jobs. Here, the record to date in high-tech firms is fairly dismal. Strong affirmative action policies are required both in the educational system and in the hiring, promotion, and training policies of high-tech employers. Ignoring affirmative action means that women, minorities, and even older men will continue to be excluded from one of the most desirable areas of job growth in the coming decades: professional/technical/scientific occupations. But since everyone cannot be employed in these fields, regardless of who get hired, we also need strong policies for 'comparable worth' and pay equity, whereby job content and skill levels of all occupations are reanalysed, redefined, and restructured to reduce the wide disparity in compensation and working conditions between different categories of employment that are today highly segregated by sex, race, and age.

If current employment trends continue, then American society is facing the prospect of a major increase in the number of 'brain workers', both in absolute numbers and particularly as a percentage of total paid employment. This prospect brings with it considerable problems of adjustment for the existing adult population. On the other hand, it also holds out the possibility of a major increase of jobs in our educational institutions as well as the possibility of greater opportunities for creative work by a larger share of the US population. Whether very large absolute increases in the number of these jobs will occur as forecast, and whether equal access to these prospective job opportunities will be ensured through vigorous public and private action, remain vital and unanswered policy questions in 1984.

Small Business vs. Large Corporate Development

American public opinion and policy-makers have often looked with great favour on small business development as an alternative to the giant corporation, and the growth of high-tech industries is frequently extolled as a successful example of small decentralized entrepreneurship. Overall, however, the growth of these industries may end up being at least as concentrated as, if not more concentrated than, any other sector of the US economy.

First of all, in other sectors where three or four firms dominate the market, such as in steel, auto, chemicals, aircraft, pharmaceuticals, petroleum, electrical machinery, rubber, and glass, there are still thousands of smaller firms that produce parts, accessories, machine tools and dies, and perform a myriad of production and service-related activities, often on subcontract from one of the majors. These smaller companies generally experience greater instability in market demand. Larger firms rely upon these suppliers and subcontractors to bear the risks of seasonal production and of new product development, and to bear the resonsibility of recruiting and laying off workers with greater cyclical fluctuation. Dominant firms in an industry frequently point to the cost savings in lower overhead and greater efficiency of subcontracting or of purchasing supplies and services from smaller companies rather than engaging in 'in-house' production. Small businesses hold their own in highly-concentrated industries only by specializing in market niches where the demand for the goods or services is not sufficiently large-scale and stable enough for giant corporations to want to compete.

High-tech industries conform to the pattern just described. In the electronics industry, for example, production of mainframe computers is highly concentrated among a small number of firms (with IBM holding near monopoly status), and in production of mini and micro computers and semiconductors and other electronic components the four- and eight-firm concentration ratios are also quite high. While initially, with the development of a new product, there may have been a good deal of competition between many small firms, the pattern of merger, consolidation, and business failure has quickly led to rather concentrated market dominance. Small business, of course, will continue to grow side-by-side with big business for the reasons cited above; in fact, behind the fabled tales of electronics industry executives splitting off from the parent company to start their own small firms, we find that in many cases, top executives who remain with the parent company are some of the principal financial backers of the new venture.

Despite the proliferation of company names on the high-tech scene, we increasingly find a significant conglomeration of actual ownership. Not only, as cited above, are the concentration ratios high in most sectors of high-tech production, but many of these large high-tech firms are being bought up by even larger multi-national conglomerate corporations. Even the new small entrepreneurial high-tech enterprises are, in many cases, already owned by giant corporations. For example, the California case studies (see pages 35–48) showed that the newly-emerging pioneers in biotechnology, robotics, and photovoltaics were actually owned by major oil, drug, and other manufacturing corporations, even where the new venture retained a separate management identity. Thus, we find that the need for start-up capital and later for expansion capital, given the costliness of research and product development, marketing and other basic expenditures, means that many of the new high-tech entrepreneurs are really just managers or professional workers for one of the *Fortune* 500 firms. Even in computer software, which does not involve huge capital costs, the Hall/Markusen/Osborn/Wachsman study (1982) found a tendency toward large corporate ownership in certain categories, a pattern of concentration similar to the merger mania still accelerating in financial and business services.

One reason for the level of concentration among the prime contractors (as opposed to the numerous subcontractors) in high-tech industries is that the US Department of Defense (DOD) is still the largest single purchaser of many of the products and services, and the largest single financier of many aspects of the research and development. The US military, which since the 1940s has played a key role in nurturing and spawning these new technologies and new private industries, still sees itself as responsible for subsidizing development of 'state-of-the-art' technologies in many key industries. The pattern of dependency of these private corporations on the Defense Department does not always receive the attention it deserves as a serious economic and public policy issue. Among other consequences of this relationship, however, is that the DOD preference for dealing primarily with very large established companies, a preference that has been reproduced by The Department of Energy in its approach to new energy-production technologies, encourages the trend toward ever higher levels of industries concentration.

Investing in People: Which People, Which Skills?

Many high-tech employment strategies focus on revamping the public role in education and research. The main thrust of these initiatives is to push for greater public and private funding of maths, science, and computer education in primary and secondary schools, and electrical engineering and computer science education in universities, including more and better technical equipment, more money for research grants and fellowships, and higher faculty salaries in certain fields. Both 'Atari Democrats' and Reagan Republicans argue that educating people for the new 'Information Age' of computers and telecommunications will meet the needs of an expanding labour force in these areas, lead to the development of new products, and expand the market for existing electronic products. Some politicians make analogies to the 'Sputnik Crisis' of 1957, which led to the passage of the National Defense Education Act (NDEA) in 1958 and major expansions in the federal military and space budgets, and which sparked a new generation of technological developments through publicly-funded research and education. In this view, the challenge of the 1980s is not to put a man on the moon, but to boost the US economic growth through the widespread development of new technologies.

It is questionable whether vigorous public promotion of the private high-tech sector even makes sense as an employment strategy, as I have indicated above. Investing in education makes sense, however, as an economic strategy, as if both creates jobs directly and acts as a crucial stimulus to indirect job creation. For example, the highly-skilled nature of the population in certain US metropolitan areas is frequently cited as a major factor in attracting and spawning new business investment and private sector employment.

The analogy to NDEA breaks down at this point, however, because in the 1960s, all forms of education and research expenditure grew at very rapid rates, whereas in the 1980s, sharp federal, state, and local budget cutbacks are the rule rather than the exception. In the context of fiscal austerity, high-tech education programmes are competing for shrinking public and private education dollars, in that funds are proposed to be shifted from other current educational programmes rather than added from increased revenues. At the same time as public policy-makers and corporate leaders are talking about the urgent need to increase faculty salaries in electrical engineering and computer science, overall educational expenditures in the United States, from kindergarten to post-doctorate, are facing severe budget reductions.

Placed in the context of the resource needs of the total education programme, these high-tech education initiatives by themselves make little sense as the main components of a long-term employment strategy. The most important characteristic of a highly-skilled workforce in an age when technology is constantly changing is the ability to think clearly, to learn quickly, and to adapt to an ever-changing workplace and consumer environment. The best way to achieve this is through strong, well-rounded basic education, of which technical knowledge and skills are just one aspect. For example, at one time, keypunch operators were needed in great quantities as a result of spreading computerization. New advances in technology will shortly turn keypunch operators into an endangered species. Narrow skill training leaves these operators unable to adapt well to other forms of data-processing employment, let alone to wider clerical or other employment fields. A good basic education in reading, verbal, and analytical skills (including maths and science), as well as 'hands-on' technical training, would be of greater benefit to these workers in their career lifespan and would be of greater benefit to prospective employers. Studies of clerical workers and productivity with new word processing and other information/communication technologies have confirmed the need for a good, broad, basic education. Such an economic policy goal can only be achieved by an overall expansion of educational resources, not by sharply cutting back in most areas in order to expand a few.

Basic education is not the only issue. Many of the high-tech education programmes are aimed at increasing certain forms of specialized training, particularly at the college level. These specializa-tions are proposed to thrive at the expence of other academic fields, which might wither and die. Such an approach, as a long-term economic/employment policy, is quite mistaken, because the hall-mark of the advancing technological revolution is the wide variety of cross-disciplinary skills and integrated knowledge necessary to de-sign, produce, and disseminate new inventions and innovations. For example, one of the biggest bottlenecks in the spread of automated/

computerized manufacturing is that people trained in electrical engineering and computer science generally are ignorant of mechanical engineering, and vice versa. Mechanical engineering has been a dying field in the 'Information Age', and yet now we discover that its neglect has left a crucial gap. In the development of computer software, the lack of which is now the single most pressing bottleneck to the spread of computer hardware, a vast array of language, logic, and communication skills, as well as very specialized non-high-tech academic training, are vital to solving problems in this industry. Putting more education dollars into computer science and cutting back on English, history, classics, linguistics, French literature, African studies, etc. could be disastrous for the needs of the 'Information Age' and the very specific requirements of the computer software industry.

Recently, two major Japanese corporations acknowledged this problem by giving major educational and research grants to two very unusual institutions from a traditional high-tech perspective: Sony's grant went to the American Film Institute for a video production studio, and Mitsui's grant went to the UCLA College of Fine Arts, 'to study, among other things, the complex problems of processing and storing the explosion of scientific and commercial information produced by an increasingly technological society'. 'There are so many things that are involved', said a Mitsui executive, 'video, animation, cable, satellite, it's very complex.' He further pointed out that the ability to produce computer hardware at present far outstrips the ability to write programs to direct the machines or to develop forms of communication and utilization by which people can employ and interact with new technologies in their daily work and community lives (*Los Angeles Times*, 1982).

Who Will Control the Development and Uses of New Technologies?

Since the spread of this knowledge-based economy will be based to a significant extent on research, a major problem arises as to: (1) who will finance the research; (2) who will control the research; (3) who will control the uses of the research findings; (4) who will benefit or suffer from these uses? The issue of scholarly, free, scientific inquiry in university microbiology departments versus the commercialization of products utilizing recombinant DNA (gene splicing) has sparked major controversy among faculty and administrations at a number of leading universities and medical schools. The Regents of the University of California recently adopted stiff guidelines on commercialization of campus-based research. Their argument is that since the educational institution is publicly-supported, the emphasis should be on broad public benefit rather than narrow private gain. And yet University of California researchers, under contract from large agricultural firms, developed an automatic tomato harvester and a 'square tomato' capable of machine harvesting. Through this research, the University budget gained by receiving grants and by royalties from a licensing agreement; the agricultural corporations gained by lowering labour costs; consumers may have gained through lower tomato prices (though this is arguable), but probably lost in tomato taste.

One group definitely lost: human tomato harvesters, farm labourers, who lost a large number of jobs due to this academically-researched technological development. These farmworkers had no part in the decision-making process either of the privately-owned (but publicly-subsidized through numerous federal and state agricultural, trade, and water policies) agri-businesses or the publicly-owned and subsidized university. No explicit public policy decision was ever made to displace these workers, and yet a private decision was made and it was subsidized with public funds. And no provision was made for the fruits of this technological change to be shared with the farm workers who were made jobless. They did not receive any share of profits from their former employers, nor any share of royalties from the University. Perhaps both would have been feasible, enabling them to organize cooperative farms, or start their own businesses or get training and education to branch out into new careers.

Clearly we cannot devise a high-tech economic policy designed to enhance the employment and income prospects of the total US population, to minimize individual and community disruption, to build democratic consensus, and to preserve the positive aspects of our physical and social environment, without raising the issue of who *controls* the development and uses of new technology.

Workers and communities will need to develop tools for negotiating and enforcing 'collective bargains' with private employers and public institutions over the introduction of new technologies so that the benefits and costs are openly assessed and equitably distributed. This could mean slowing down *or* accelerating the pace of change – in fact it will probably mean both, depending on the circumstances. But it definitely means that all who are affected will have an opportunity to negotiate over what they are giving up, and strike a private or public contractual bargain over what they will get in return. In the absence of such a process, a government policy of investing heavily in high tech may bring economic chaos, not salvation.

References

Bluestone, Barry and Harrison, Bennett (1982) *The Deindustrialization of America*. New York: Basic Books.

Business Week (1981) The Speedup in Automation. 3 August.

Center for the Continuing Study of the California Economy (1982) *The California Economy: 1970–1990*. Sacramento: Department of Economic and Business Development.

Feldman, Marshall and O'Malley, Elizabeth (1982) *California's Biotechnology Industry*. Sacramento: California Commission on Industrial Innovation.

Hall, Peter, Markusen, Ann, Osborne, Richard and Wachsman, Barbara (1982) *The California Software Industry: Problems and Prospects*. Sacramento: California Commission on Industrial Innovation.

Los Angeles Times (1982) Part V, P. 1, 16 October; Part IX, P. 1, 18 November.

7

High-technology industries and agglomeration economies

RAY OAKEY

*What is the evidence for agglomeration
economies in the high-tech industries of Silicon
Valley and what may be learned from a comparison
of such economies in Silicon Valley with those
in South East England and Scotland?*

High-Technology Industry, Product Life Cycles and the Principle of Agglomeration

Silicon Valley has gained an irrevocable place in the vocabularies of a wide range of academics, journalists, and politicians concerned with industrial location and regional economic development. Indeed, the worldwide interest of the media has widened knowledge of this area and its industries to a larger non-professional audience. But such commentators have frequently exaggerated the novel attributes of Silicon Valley to an extent where the layman might believe that few similarities exist between these new forms of production and more traditional methods of manufacture such as textiles or motor vehicles. For example, emphasis on space-age technologies often overstates the, admittedly important, role of the research scientist and his non-conformist work patterns at the expense of many skilled and semi-skilled shopfloor workers who labour on the downstream production phases of the high-technology industrial manufacturing process (Oakey, 1981). The tasks of these, often female, workers are similar to those performed in less glamorous industries such as textiles or electrical consumer goods. These employment similarities, and the undeniable need of high-technology firms to add value to input materials through manufacture, and dispatch outputs to customers, suggests that there may remain scope for the application of traditional concepts of location theory to an explanation of the new industrial growth in high technology industrial areas.

Any attempt to apply the basic principles of location theory to a consideration of the rapid development of Silicon Valley over the past thirty years must inevitably consider the relevance of the long-standing principle of industrial agglomeration (Weber, 1909). There is considerable evidence from previous studies that material and information advantages have produced agglomeration economies for often vertically disintegrated, but spatially concentrated, forms of production. If agglomeration economies have helped to explain the past clustering of the gun and jewellery industry (Wise, 1949), furniture manufacture (Hall, 1962) and instruments production (Martin, 1966), agglomeration forces might also explain the current clustering of high-technology industry in Silicon Valley today.

The implication that high-technology industry is heavily agglomerated will be closely considered below in the light of relevant evidence. These selected data are derived from a more detailed survey designed to investigate the impact of agglomeration advantage by noting the varying quality of local regional resource inputs on technical innovation within high-technology small firms (Oakey, 1984). Vigorous technical innovation in a given region is a major determinant of manufacturing growth (Freeman, 1974; Feller, 1975) and may imply subsequent local agglomeration advantage provided by high-quality local resources. The following analysis will use a broad definition of local resource (or agglomeration) advantage to include, not only local material linkages (Weber, 1909; Smith, 1970), but also the benefits of local information linkages (Wood, 1969), a rich supply of local labour (Gilmour, 1974), and the stimulus of locally-available investment capital (Estall, 1972; Little, 1977; Bullock, 1983). However, in advance of these empirical investigations, a brief explanation of the means by which the data were obtained is indicated.

The methodological Approach

At a general level, the detection of agglomeration advantage in a known concentration of high-technology production, such as Silicon Valley, presents several methodological problems. Clearly, in order that agglomeration advantage might be measured, it was essential that a control region (or regions) should be studied. Hence, the two economically diverse British regions of South East England and Scotland were chosen to contrast with the Bay Area of California, which is dominated by the industrial production of Silicon Valley (Oakey, 1984). South East England has been consistently Britain's most successful region since the Second World War, while Scotland is a development region with severe problems of industrial decline in older heavy industries.

The California data derive from a geographical area of similar size to the British regions, and is centred on the San Francisco Bay, extending from Healdsberg in the north to Monterey in the south, and eastward to the foot of the Sierra mountains (see figure 1). However, in terms of the study industries, the dominance of Silicon Valley and its immediate environs is aparent from figure 7.1, where 48 per cent of the firms randomly sampled from the total region were located within Silicon Valley, while 77 per cent were located within a 50 km circle centred on Silicon Valley, and 91 per cent located on or near the shores of San Francisco Bay. Although Silicon Valley is a major influence on the survey data presented below, the term Bay Area will be used in the following empirical sections and conclusion since agglomeration advantage, should it exist, will extend beyond the immediate limits of Silicon Valley to include other Bay Area locales in immediately adjacent areas.

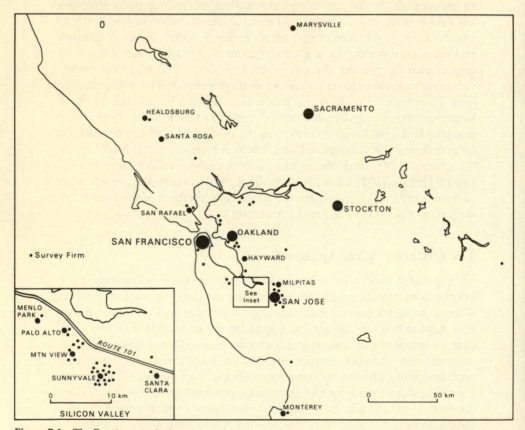

Figure 7.1   The Bay Area, including Silicon Valley. Constituent counties are as follows: Alameda, Contra Costa, Marin, Monterey, Napa, Nevada, Sacramento, San Benito, San Francisco, San Joaquin, San Mateo, Santa Clara, Santa Cruz, Sonoma, Stanislaus.

Since the research sought to explore the extent to which local agglomeration advantages promoted innovation and growth in the firm, it was decided that the most sensitive 'litmus test' of such conduciveness should be obtained through the study of totally *independent* small high-technology instrument and electronic firms. (For full details of the British and US product group chosen, see appendix.) Such reasoning derived first from the stringent technological demands that these firms place on local input resources (for example, material inputs, labour); and second, from the greater local orientation of such firms when compared with branch plants of similar size, which have access to a wider range of non-local corporate resources (Oakey, 1979a). The following data on regional variations in agglomeration advantage are derived from a questionnaire interview survey of 174 firms, comprising 60 Bay Area, 60 South Eastern and 54 Scottish enterprises. The information was obtained during 1981 in Britain and 1982 in the United States. For further details of the methodology, directory sources and sampling procedure see Oakey (1984).

The Evidence

In this analysis of local agglomeration advantage, a recurrent theme will be the investigation of whether local resource advantages cause a superior level of innovation in the Bay Area to that of the British control regions. It is clear from table 7.1 that product innovation in

Table 7.1   The incidence of new product innovation by region.

New Product Innovation	Scotland		Region South East		Bay Area	
N = 174	N	%	N	%	N	%
Innovation	34	(63.0)	47	(78.3)	51	(85.0)
None	20	(37.0)	13	(21.7)	9	(15.0)
Total	54	(100.0)	60	(100.0)	60	(100.0)

Chi-square = 7.84 $p = 0.019$

survey firms, for the five-year period prior to interview, supports the general contention that the Bay Area is the most innovative region, and that Scotland, the British development region, is the laggard. At the level of the individual firm, product innovation is readily distinguishable from process improvement since the former relates to improvements in the technology of outputs while the latter is concerned with the technology of their production (Oakey, 1981). There was a 22 per cent difference in the product innovation performance of these two regions, while the South East fell between the two extremes. The investigation of agglomeration advantage begins with a consideration of local linkages.

Agglomeration Advantages and Linkages

In advance of the data, it is helpful to clarify the general nature of inputs and outputs. The bulk of material inputs and outputs referred to below are semi-finished goods at various points in a chain of production which links 'true' raw materials to 'true' finished products. Typically a survey firm will add value to a mixture of purchased components and sub-contracted sub-assemblies to produce a 'product' which may itself be a sub-assembly in a larger customer firm.

Previous arguments suggest, and empirical research into high-technology industry confirms, that input and output linkages in high-technology forms of production are generally large in number and national and international in distribution (Oakey, 1981). Because of the relatively high value of inputs and outputs, transport costs are a small proportion of the total price to customers. Thus, both because of insignificant transport costs and the frequently wide spread of suppliers and customers, it might be argued that the small number of input and output linkages of *local* origin in an agglomeration is unlikely to enhance significantly the innovation performance of high-technology firms when compared with those in other locations.

However, high-technology firms may be linked to their suppliers and customers, not only by the overt flows of materials to and from the plant, but by significant information feedback loops to suppliers and from customers. Although materials may pass over long distances in such relationships with few transport diseconomies, the effect of distance on information feedback may be more locationally sensitive (Robertson, 1974). Other work has shown the value of the close proximity of vendors and customers of services where face to face contact promotes more frequent and fruitful information exchange (Goddard, 1978). Hence, a worthy hypothesis might argue that, while a few transport economies result from the close proximity of high-technology firms, subtle advantages to innovation are gained from local information exchange through 'feedback loops'. This potential will be explored below for both input and output linkages, in turn.

Input linkages.   In order to establish the extent of local material input sourcing, survey firm respondents were asked to estimate the proportion of their total material inputs (by value) derived from within 30 miles (50km) of the plant. It is clear from table 7.2 that there is a sharp difference between the local purchasing of Bay Area firms and

Table 7.2 Percent purchased locally (within 30 miles) by region.

Percent Input	Scotland		South East		Bay Area	
N = 174	N	%	N	%	N	%
Nil	8	(14.8)	10	(16.7)	7	(11.7)
1–24	34	(63.0)	27	(45.0)	8	(13.3)
25–49	6	(11.1)	12	(20.0)	4	(6.7)
50–74	2	(3.7)	7	(11.2)	17	(28.3)
75–99	3	(5.6)	4	(6.7)	22	(36.7)
100	1	(1.9)	0	(0.0)	2	(3.3)
Total	54	(100.0)	60	(100.0)	60	(100.0)

Chi-square 59.35 $p = 0.0001$

their Scottish counterparts. While a mere 11 per cent of Scottish firms purchased over 50 per cent of their material inputs locally, the equivalent figure for Bay Area firms was 68 per cent, while the South Eastern firms recorded an 18 per cent level. This sharp regional contrast is confirmed by a chi-square test on table 7.2 that easily exceeds the $p = 0.001$ level of significance. Clearly, the regions differ structurally and physically in several respects that may partly explain this pattern of results. Ironically, the low level of local sourcing in the South East of England may be partly caused by the relative size of the region. For although the South East is small in comparison with California, it is large when compared with the concentration of Bay Area industry. Hence, many South Eastern suppliers would not have fallen within the 50-km radius encircling the survey plants, and have thus been excluded from table 7.2. However, the very high incidence of local sourcing in the Bay Area is valid evidence of a *physically intense* concentration of sophisticated high-technology material inputs. This high level of local sourcing must reflect the range and quality of high-technology suppliers in this tight-knit industrial concentration. Indeed, it should be remembered that Silicon Valley firms, which comprise 48 per cent of all Bay Area firms, are contained within a rectangular area that measures no more than 20km by 10km (see figure 7.1). Moreover, beyond the obvious physical convenience of such sourcing arrangements, the subtle technical information benefits for innovation from such close liaison with suppliers on frequently changing product design is likely to promote the high level of Bay Area product innovation in table 7.1.

However, this possible association was tested in a converse manner by examining the extent to which survey firms found that their local supply relationships directly inhibited innovation. Survey firm executives were asked if a poor level of local services to their production process, in terms of material suppliers, sub-contracting and services to production machinery, directly inhibited innovation by their business. Of the 19 firms acknowledging this problem, 14 were located in Scotland, comprising 26 per cent of the Scottish total, compared with 2 per cent for the South East and 7 per cent for the Bay Area. The cause of the problem divided almost equally between poor choice of stockists and deficiencies in local sub-contracting facilities. This evidence reinforces the previous interpretation of table 7.2 in that the noted lower use of local material inputs by Scottish firms must be partly explained by these inhibitions. Such combined results imply that a concentration of local suppliers may aid innovation and provide agglomeration advantage in the small high-technology firm, while a poor level of local input services may inhibit innovation and subsequent growth.

Output linkages   In a similar manner to the approach adopted for input linkages, respondents in the three study regions were asked to estimate the percentage of their sales (by value) they dispatched to customers within 30 miles of their plant. However, unlike inputs, there was little evidence of a predominantly local orientation of output links in any of the study regions. For example, the percentages of firms with over 50 per cent of their sales in the local area for Scotland, South East England and the Bay Area were 21 per cent, 27 per cent and 34 per cent respectively. Notably, the difference in these figures between Scotland and the Bay Area is not great, and unlike the similar data for input linkages, where the chi-square test exceeded the $p = 0.001$ level (table 7.1), the value for table 7.3 was an insignificant $p = 0.31$. These results suggest, and further investigations confirm, that there is little local agglomeration advantage from technical information feedback from customers. Indeed, the passage of *significant* technical information from customers was rare for *both* local and non-local customers (Oakey, 1984).

Table 7.3   Percent sold locally (within 30 miles) by region.

Percent Sold Locally	Scotland		Region South East		Bay Area	
$N = 173$	N	%	N	%	N	%
Nil	10	(18.9)	4	(6.7)	8	(13.3)
1–24	28	(52.3)	30	(50.0)	27	(45.0)
25–49	4	(7.5)	10	(16.7)	5	(8.3)
50–74	4	(7.5)	5	(8.3)	10	(16.7)
75–99	7	(13.2)	11	(18.3)	9	(15.0)
100	0	(0.0)	0	(0.0)	1	(1.7)
Total	53	(100.0)	60	(100.0)	60	(100.0)

Chi-square = 11.50 $p = 0.311$

Agglomeration Economies and Technical Information

Detailed analysis elsewhere has indicated that 148 (85 per cent) of the small high-technology firms in this survey maintained some form of internal research and development effort (Oakey, 1984). Consequently, the general value of externally acquired technical information must largely support the overall *internal* research and development of the firm. Nonetheless, it is true that an externally available source of technical information, such as a university, *might* give a significant boost to the internal research and development effort of small high-technology firms. Indeed, it has been argued by writers in the United States that the concentration of high-technology industry in both the Route 128 area near Boston and the Silicon Valley complex south of San Francisco owe much to the stimulation of technically oriented universities in the vicinity (Deuterman, 1966; Gibson, 1970; Cooper, 1970).

However, many of the assertions on technical links between universities and local industrial firms depend on concommitance rather than direct causality. It is often assumed that because local firms with technical needs, and universities with relevant expertise, are juxtaposed, then interaction occurs. But detailed evidence on the extent of links between high-technology scientific instruments firms and universities in Britain has indicated that contacts were infrequent and of a supportive nature when they occurred (Oakey, 1979*b*). Clearly, the current survey is an ideal opportunity to shed some light on possible international differences in the technical links of small firms with external research institutions.

Survey firm establishments were asked if their firms maintained any external contact with a source of technical information of importance in developing products and processes in the plant. Surprisingly, Bay Area firms recorded the lowest level of external research and development links, with only 14 firms (23 per cent) acknowledging a link compared with approximately half the Scottish and South East England sub-samples (table 7.4). Local universities

Table 7.4 The incidence of important technical information contacts by region.

| Technical | Region | | | | | |
contacts	Scotland		South East		Bay Area	
N = 173	N	%	N	%	N	%
Important contacts	30	(55.6)	25	(42.4)	14	(23.3)
No important contacts	24	(44.4)	34	(57.6)	46	(76.7)
Total	54	(100.0)	59	(100.0)	60	(100.0)

Chi-square = 12.54 $p = 0.002$

played an important part in producing the higher level of contact in Scotland. However, there appears to be little correlation between the most innovative Bay Area region (table 7.1) and extensive local or national links with external research institutions. An attempt was made to ascertain the strength of the information flow in the minority of firms with a technical link to an outside body. Firm executives were asked if the breaking of the information flow, for whatever reason, would cause serious disruption to their internal innovation performance. A very small minority of only 6 Scottish, 4 South Eastern and 3 Bay Area firms responded affirmatively to this question.

These data give a clear overall impression that external technical information links are not profuse, nor are those that do exist of great significance to internal innovation in survey firms. The impression created by the previous literature (Deuterman, 1966; Cooper, 1970) that American firms might maintain more abundant and technically important links with local and national technical universities is found to be false in the Bay Area sub-sample. Indeed, this result is particularly striking given that a large number of Bay Area firms were located in Silicon Valley, no more than 10 kilometres from Stanford University.

Agglomeration Advantage and Labour

The shortage of labour in any given local economy is an effect that may ensue from one of two major causes. First, taking a depressed region example, labour shortages can occur where the supply of a particular type of worker is low. In those high-technology industries that do exist in such regions, shortage of skilled workers may cause labour problems, predominantly because a moderate demand is not met by an inferior supply. Often this problem confronts large foreign firms seeking to locate a branch plant in one of Britain's development regions. Since training is not practicable in the short term, the immediate dearth of suitable high-technology skills in the depressed region repels the potential locator, thus helping to perpetuate an inferior regional skill structure (Oakey, 1983). Second, at the other extreme, labour shortages may occur in areas where high-technology industry is agglomerated when a large high-technology skilled labour market acts as a retentive force for existing firms and an attractive force for other companies from outside the agglomeration. In these circumstances, labour shortages are caused by a large local skilled workforce being unable to satisfy the greater demand of local firms. The manner in which firms acquire or increase their workforces in such an area is by outbidding their fellow firms, thus causing escalating wage levels and higher production costs. These comments are relevant to the following consideration of the agglomeration advantages of labour in the study regions.

Labour shortages   Respondents were asked if they had recently experienced shortages of any particular type of labour in their local area. It was generally evident from the overall pattern of responses that the more prosperous and innovative South East of England and Bay Area regions displayed a greater propensity to acknowledge labour shortages, with 58 per cent and 48 per cent respective levels of labour shortage acknowledged, compared with 37 per cent for Scotland. A chi-square test on these results when tabulated yielded a significance level of $p = 0.111$, marginally outside the normally accepted $p = 0.05$ level. It is notable that Scotland, the least innovative region, records the lowest level of labour shortage. Given the other evidence on the lower product innovation performance of Scotland in table 7.1, and elsewhere (Oakey *et al.*, 1980, 1982), it is doubtful whether the lower level of problems with labour supply in are caused by a particularly comprehensive labour supply meeting vigorous *innovation led* demand. It is more likely that a poor labour supply remains adequate to suffice the relatively low level of demand from high-technology firms in Scotland.

However, a closer examination of the skill type shortages acknowledged by firms with labour problems yielded detailed evidence of further interest. Significantly, there was a difference in the types of labour shortage in Scotland compared with the other regions. While numbers in individual cells are small, it is clear that research and development personnel constituted the main category of shortage in Scotland, while shopfloor skilled and semi-skilled workers combined were overwhelmingly the cause of shortages in the more prosperous South East and the Bay Areas (table 7.5). The difference between Scotland and the other regions was confirmed by a chi-square test which was strongly significant at the $p = 0.05$ level.

Table 7.5   The regional distribution of skill shortages.

Shortage Type	Scotland		South East		Bay Area	
$N = 80$	N	%	N	%	N	%
R&D worker	8	(40.0)	2	(6.1)	3	(11.1)
Skilled shopfloor worker	5	(25.0)	17	(51.5)	17	(63.0)
Shopfloor worker	3	(15.0)	11	(33.3)	4	(14.8)
Other	4	(20.0)	3	(9.1)	3	(11.1)
Total	20	(100.0)	33	(100.0)	27	(100.0)

Chi square = 17.15 $p = 0.009$

Firm executives acknowledging shortages of labour were questioned to pinpoint specifically whether such differences had inhibited their efforts towards product innovation. The results of this question may be seen as a further development of the trend hinted at in table 7.5. As might be expected from the previous evidence, labour was less of an inhibitor of product innovation in the Scottish instance. The Scottish region, which possessed the lowest proportion of firms with labour shortages, also recorded the lowest proportion of firms acknowledging that labour shortages inhibited product innovation, with a 10 per cent level of affirmative responses among those firms with labour problems, compared with larger 41 per cent and 48 per cent levels for the South East and Bay Area firms respectively. These sharp differences between the three regions were confirmed by a chi-square test, on the tabulated data, significant at the $p = 0.02$ level. This result reflects the increased regional differences between labour shortages *per se* noted above, in which a weaker significance of $p = 0.111$ was achieved, and the current direct investigation of the impact of such shortages on innovation in survey firms.

Agglomeration Economies and Investment Capital

Since the central theme of this chapter is the examination of the effect of local agglomeration economies on innovation and subsequent prosperity in survey firms, it might be expected that variations in the availability of local external investment capital for expanding small high-technology firms might influence the extent and pace of innovation and growth. The regions studied are well suited to this task since they are individual examples of diverse financial environments, ranging from the public-sector assisted development region of Scotland, through the British unassisted area of South East England, to the Bay Area of California, perhaps the modern home of venture capitalism (Little, 1977; Bullock, 1983). Indeed, these international data offer the opportunity to evaluate the contribution of venture capital to the impressive small firm growth found in the Silicon Valley area of California, and compare such benefits with evidence from the British regions. The analysis begins with an investigation of sources of start-up capital in new survey firms, since agglomeration is enhanced, not only by the growth of existing firms, but also by the contribution of new fast-growing firms to the local economy.

Sources of start-up capital   Regional evidence on the initial main source of start-up capital indicates the universal popularity of personal savings as a means of beginning a firm. The 63 per cent average level of acknowledgement for this source is similar to levels observed in other studies of small firm 'start-up' finance (Cross, 1981; Storey, 1982). While a wide range of other sources are sparsely represented, the only other important origin of start-up funds is private venture capital (table 7.6). This is the first sign that the much vaunted capital market in

Table 7.6   Sources of start-up capital in firms founded since 1970 by region.

Start up Capital	Scotland		South East		Bay Area	
N = 73	N	%	N	%	N	%
Personal savings	20	(67.0)	11	(69.0)	14	(52.0)
Previous assets	0	(0.0)	2	(12.0)	2	(7.0)
Bank loan	2	(7.0)	1	(6.0)	1	(4.0)
Second mortgage	1	(3.0)	0	(0.0)	1	(4.0)
Venture capital	1	(3.0)	1	(6.0)	8	(30.0)
Other	6	(20.0)	1	(6.0)	1	(4.0)
Total	30	(100.0)	16	(100.0)	27	(100.0)

the Bay Area might be producing regionally different results within the total survey sample. Although numbers are relatively small, eight (30 per cent) of the Bay Area firms founded since 1970 were aided in their birth by venture capital, while this source was negligible in the British regions.

Sources of investment finance   Survey firms were further asked to indicate the main source of investment finance in their business over the five-year period prior to interview. As noted in the case of new firm start-up, it is no surprise to discover from table 7.7 that there is an

Table 7.7   Main capital investment sources by region.

Capital Sources	Scotland		South East		Bay Area	
N = 174	N	%	N	%	N	%
Internal profits	35	(64.8)	49	(81.7)	45	(75.0)
Local bank	13	(24.1)	5	(8.3)	6	(10.0)
Venture capital	1	(1.9)	2	(3.3)	9	(15.0)
Other	5	(9.3)	4	(6.7)	0	(0.0)
Total	54	(100.0)	60	(100.0)	60	(100.0)

overwhelming tendency in all regions to move forward incrementally on the basis of internal profits when funding the main investment needs of the firm, although there is a higher level of bank funding in the Scottish instance. However, the overall impression from these results would suggest that, since the major source of investment capital is *internal* profits, any agglomeration advantage from local sources of external investment capital is minimal in South East England, dependent on local bank funding in Scotland, and mainly characterized by venture capital funding in the Bay Area. Further comments on the conceptual and policy implications of the marginal role of venture capital funding in the Bay Area are reserved for the conclusion.

Conclusion

Agglomeration Economies in the Bay Area – A Summary of Results

Clearly this chapter has not exhausted *all* the local economic advantages that might constitute agglomeration economies. However, it is argued that the factors considered are major potential contributors to local agglomeration advantage insofar as they are strong promoters of internal innovation and growth within manufacturing firms. The specific factors that might constitute agglomeration economies are grouped together below and considered in terms of those that did not appear to yield agglomeration economies in the Bay Area, and those that appeared to offer agglomeration advantage in this area when compared with the British control regions. The impact of labour will be dealt with separately, since its effects are not straightforward.

Insignificant factors Unlike traditional agglomerations, output linkages to customers did not seem to offer particular local agglomeration economies to survey firms in general, nor Bay Area firms in particular. The substantial proportion of output exported from the Bay Area to distant national locations or abroad, while not negating an important minority of local sales, reflected the wide spread of customers for the specialist outputs of high-technology industrial production (Oakey 1981, 1984). While sales to other firms in the Bay Area perform a useful function (as comments on input linkages below will imply), the *bulk* of sales in any high-technology firm will be broadly spread, thus reducing any local agglomeration advantage to the firm through technical interaction with local customers. Because the technology embodied in products sold by high-technology firms is predominantly developed 'in house' with *internal* research and development, long distance customer linkages can be maintained, often with few technical problems for the supplier firm.

Consequently, it was not surprising to discover that the small Bay Area firms of the study maintained the lowest regional level of contacts with local universities. Bay Area interviewees frequently stressed that their technical capacity was totally 'in house' and that they believed universities would not be able to offer technical help for innovation in their highly-specialized production niche. Since there is evidence to support the view that innovation in the small firm is enhanced by a flexible internal work environment (Rothwell and Zegveld, 1982), the unimportance of external technical information should be no surprise. However, these comments on *small* firms should be qualified by the acknowledgement that more formal and large-scale contract research programmes may exist between Stanford and Berkeley universities and larger Silicon Valley corporations (Gibson, 1970).

Significant factors Unlike output linkages, there was evidence to suggest that the high proportion of local input linkage sourcing produced agglomeration advantages for firms in Silicon Valley. Indeed, the executives of 8 firms (14 per cent) in Silicon Valley mentioned the quality of local input suppliers as the single most important factor in their location (Oakey, 1984). For while the majority of Bay Area firms' output is not locally consumed, it is clearly helpful for high-technology firms in an agglomeration to have access to a wide range of specialist *local* suppliers. Significantly, unlike outputs, any input that is purchased implies that there is no internal technical capacity with which to produce the item concerned. Hence, since the technical capacity lies in the supplier firm, the proximity of such a vendor facilitates interaction on new inputs to rapidly changing product designs in the small consumer firms of this study. Certainly, the paucity of input suppliers of materials and sub-contract firms was significantly missed in the Scottish instance.

The preceding results put in context many of the myths surrounding the importance of venture capital. It may be recalled that 30 per cent of the new firms founded in the Bay Area since 1970 were established with venture capital, while 15 per cent of the Bay Area sample acknowledged that venture capital was a main source of investment finance during the previous five years. These statistics compare with a virtual absence of any private venture capital sourcing in the British regions. Thus it is clear that the impact of venture capital is *limited* in small high-technology firms in the Bay Area and not evident on the scale that many media commentators would suggest. This view is confirmed by other recent research (Bullock, 1983).

However, there is much anecdotal evidence among Silicon Valley entrepreneurs that venture capitalists are particularly good at 'picking winners'. Because many of the venture capitalists are ex-businessmen, with technical training and business acumen, they are eminently qualified to judge both the business skills of potential recipients of venture capital *and* the technical viability of the product development for which it is sought. Since the venture capitalists are the individuals with the purse-strings, they are able to advance money quickly once they have made a decision. It is notable that the three fastest growing new firms in the survey came from the Bay Area and were all founded on venture capital and reliant on venture capital for their subsequent growth. The employment growth in these firms far exceeded any of the new firm growth in Britain (Oakey, 1984).

At an aggregate regional level, the efforts of local venture capitalists were beneficial to high-technology agglomerations in two major ways. First, although overall use of venture capitalists may not be extensive, they broaden the potential range of external capital investment sources for industrialists looking for investment finance which may be particularly relevant to firms with *rapid* growth potential. Second, since most venture capitalists are 'local men', they are more likely to plough back their profits into new businesses in the same local agglomeration. Since their main expertise lies in knowing what is being developed locally there is every likelihood that they will restrict their investments, and hence level of risk, to known local industries. Hence, venture capitalists may be seen as an integral part of the high-technology business agglomeration since they reduce capital 'leakage' by recycling the profits from previous local enterprise.

Labour and agglomeration The relevance of local labour supply to agglomeration economies is not straightforward. Survey evidence suggests that Scotland, the least innovative region, had least labour problems in terms of shopfloor workers. However, it is likely that the higher incidence of labour shortages in the South East of England and the Bay Area derives from a relatively large regional pool of high-technology labour being insufficient to keep pace with an even greater demand. Such a local demand largely stems from innovation that, in turn, derives from a concentration of *employed* skilled labour and other local agglomeration economies. Hence, local shopfloor labour shortages are largely the price of success. Ironically, labour shortages and high labour costs have always been acknowledged as a bearable by-product of 'overheating' in agglomerations (Alonso, 1970). The willingness of firms to suffer labour shortages and high wage costs in Silicon Valley is, in a sense, 'proof' of other compensatory agglomeration advantages. Indeed, although a location within high-technology industrial agglomerations may escalate wage costs for employers, higher wages may ameliorate the problems of inflated living costs (for example, high-cost housing) for white collar research and development staff. For example, since Silicon Valley offers opportunities for 'job-hopping' and a stimulating general work environment in both technical and physical terms, it is not surprising that shortages in this category of worker were lowest in the more attractive South East England and Bay Area regions.

Product Life Cycles and High-Technology Production

The preceding paragraphs have isolated local resource factors that appear to enhance innovation in the small high-technology firms in the Bay Area of California. From a material viewpoint, the importance of diverse input sources and investment capital in the Bay Area provides significant marginal advantages to production, while in terms of human resources, the presence of a large highly-skilled labour pool, although not beneficial in all respects, is nonetheless an overall contribution to agglomeration economies, both through the contribution of local skills as inputs to the high-technology innovation and production process, and as a potential source of new innovators who begin 'spin-off' firms. The following paragraphs seek to explain the effects of these individual advantages by placing them in a more general conceptual framework. This conceptualization relies heavily on product life cycle theory (Vernon, 1966).

It is generally asserted that the shape of curves achieved in the course of a product life cycle will much depend on the technological sophistication of the industry in which a product is developed. If the example of the medium-technology consumer electronics industry is taken, then the 30-year product cycle indicated in figure 7.2(a) might be typical for an electronic consumer durable, albeit with appropriate facelifts. The evolution of the product life cycle of figure 7.2(a) involves three major production phases. First, in the early stages (Stage 1), there will be many teething problems with the product surrounding its design and initial construction. This development stage requires substantial inputs of both skilled research and development and skilled shopfloor technicians. In these early stages the manufacture of the product is likely to be most efficiently located in an industrial agglomeration in order that links might be maintained with a headquarters or research and development centre commonly located in such an area (Goddard and Smith, 1978; Buswell and Lewis, 1970), and in order that recurrent changes in labour and material inputs may be met by a rich and flexible local resource environment.

During the period of maximum sales (Stage 2) it is argued that the production methods related to the product are perfected and the level of skilled-labour input, both in terms of research and development and shopfloor workers is reduced. In addition, the standardization of the product also enables material inputs to be standardized and

(a)

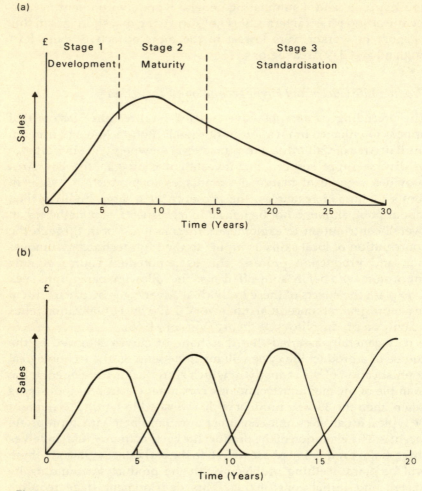

(b)

Figure 7.2   Diverse industrial product life cycles.

purchased in bulk on a regular basis. Thus, during Stage 3, the product becomes 'footloose', and may be transferred to a peripheral location where development grants and cheaper unskilled (probably female) labour may be obtained to prolong life through the reduction of production costs (Luttrell, 1962; Townroe, 1971). Production continues in this location until eventual obsolescence is reached after the 30-year cycle. The standardized electrical and mechanical engineering manufacture transferred to the British development areas in the 1960s, the keenness of firms in this type of manufacture to obtain government grants towards the purchase of capital equipment used in standardized production, and the propensity for the employment of unskilled female workers, suggests the 'Stage 3' nature of much of this mobile production (Keeble, 1976; Smith, 1979). Moreover, it is clear that there is scope in certain areas of high-technology production for a degree of type 2a standardization to take place where large firms dominate (for example, calculators, electronic toys). Indeed much of this production has been relocated from Silicon Valley to the peripheral parts of the United States and abroad.

But significantly, in terms of the current conceptualization, it is argued that the above phenomena do not apply to product cycles in many of the newest expanding high-technology industries where there remains scope for the small firm. Again using the product life cycle concept, it is clear from figure 7.2(b) that the life cycles for many high-technology products are much shorter. Life cycles in these industries may be five years in duration. The major difference between the hypothesized cycles of figures 7.2(a) and (b) is the absence of a tail (Stage 3) in figure 7.2(b). Here, this tail is replaced by a decline that is virtually the mirror image of the incline. Sales and subsequent profits are maintained by a series of multiple product life cycles, often from initial new firm start-ups, that ensure overall survival and growth. Moreover, these short product life cycles enable small firms to gain a foothold in expanding high-technology markets when economic barriers for entry are low. While many of these firms will stagnate, be absorbed or die in subsequent years, the rapid growth of several notable American small firms into large corporations over recent years confirms the potential for growth in a minority of fast growing small firms (Morse, 1976; Rothwell and Zegveld, 1982).

Several locationally important implications arise from an excited rate of product innovation, creating location behaviour that is the antithesis of that noted in figure 7.2(a) where there existed a standardized phase of production enabling large-scale production and subsequent mobility. First, it is argued that the rapid cycles rarely allow for the product to be standardized and thus become conducive to long-term mass production runs. Second, and following on from the inapplicability of mass production, there is likely to be a continuing dependence on skilled shopfloor workers. Third, because product innovation is a continuing process, figure 7.2(b) implies that the input of research and development personnel is constantly required since, no sooner has an existing product been released from the prototype stage, than another replacement product is placed on the drawing board. Fourth, since these products occur in high-technology industry, their 'raw material' inputs are commonly complicated and specialized components and sub-assemblies. Hence, the frequency of product cycles suggests that a locally available range and choice of such suppliers is desirable to cater for early radical design changes, as was argued in Stage 1 of figure 7.2(a).

Thus, this conceptualization suggests that the products of example 2b rarely evolve much past the development stage of 2a – certainly not in terms of becoming indifferent to the advantages of local agglomeration economies common in the standardization phase of figure 7.2(a). Hence, the above arguments suggest that the concentration of high-technology industry in Silicon Valley constitutes an agglomeration in a traditional sense, similar to the previously described urban agglomerated industries of the past. Such advantages are valuable to large and small firms engaged in the short product life cycles of figure 7.2(b), *and* to large firms engaged in the initial stages of long product life cycles noted in figure 7.2(a), *before* they become standardized and relocated to peripheral regions.

Certainly, the noted importance of local input linkages and labour supports the concept of locational inertia created by agglomeration advantage. Moreover, because innovation in small high-technology firms is an intrinsically *internal* process, local external technical information was unimportant. However, since internal innovation must be fuelled by investment capital, locally available investment capital in the Bay Area proved to be an agglomeration advantage since it facilitated vigorous *internal* small firm innovation.

The high technology industrial agglomeration: prospects for sustained prosperity Evidence of past agglomerations suggest that agglomeration economies tend to increase as the agglomeration grows and aggravate disparities between this area and other industrial regions increase. Agglomeration economies largely explain the concentration of Victorian industries such as cotton textiles into specialist areas, now in decline in many Western economies. However, mention of past industrial agglomeration raises a pertinent element of doubt over the prospects for future high-technology industrial growth in industrial complexes such as Silicon Valley. For example, it might be argued that the present 'boom' areas of high-technology industrial expansion will be the declining industrial problem areas of tomorrow. Indeed, at the height of textile production in Lancashire or New England, there was little anticipation of their recent dramatic decline.

A consideration of the long-term sustainability of high-technology industrial agglomerations may be addressed by a return to the product life cycle concept. It is a useful contribution to the current discussion of agglomeration, however, to view product life cycles at a macro sectoral level in which the individual products of specific high-technology electronics firms can be aggregated into a general product category for the whole industry in much the same way as the woollen textile industry is an aggregation of individual products such as worsteds or tweeds. At this aggregate level the industry-led product life cycle remains similar to that of the single firm with phases of development, maturity and decline.

The acknowledgement of the propulsive effects on sectoral growth from technological innovation is the key to an understanding of the works of great theoretical economists such as Kondratieff (1935) and Perroux (1955). However, it is central to the current argument to note that these industrial sectors have often been *physically* concentrated to reap agglomeration economies in regions that have frequently suffered when the upward movement and crest of their industry level product life cycle was followed by maturity and subsequent decline. This decline in sales may either result from approaching product obsolescence, or from the competition of more efficient producers elsewhere as in the case of cotton textiles. England abounds with industrial areas that were founded on the propulsive effect of Kondratieff's steam-driven innovation wave of the nineteenth century, only to face acute problems of industrial decline in the late twentieth century. Hence, the historical evidence on the long-term survivability of industrial agglomerations would not appear to augur well for the new high-technology industrial concentrations.

However, perhaps the most encouraging evidence to indicate that new high-technology industrial agglomerations are less likely to fail is their greater capacity to create new industries with which to ensure continued survival and growth. The common feature of all the high-technology industries is their uniformly strong commitment to research and development. This intense research and development input, both at the level of the individual high-technology firm, and at an aggregate level of the local economy when they are agglomerated, promotes rapid technological change through the acquisition of new leading edge technology, either through indigenous development in the agglomeration, or through the attraction into the area of externally discovered ideas. The high quality of the development and production workers in high-technology agglomerations is an attractive force to any external entrepreneur seeking a location to develop a high-technology product.

The evolution of industries based on new techniques, from silicon-based semiconductors to bio-engineering technologies, seems to ensure the growth of high-technology agglomerations in the foreseeable future due to the regenerative effect of new industry level product life cycles on the agglomeration. Hence, the great potential of high-technology industrial agglomerations, such as Silicon Valley, does not stem from agglomeration economies derived from a single industry such as cotton textiles or steel, but from the output of a highly skilled research and development and production workforce which can create and adapt to totally new technical innovations and production concepts. Thus, it is less likely that these new agglomerations will suffer the problems of innovation stagnation and subsequent decline common to their historical predecessors. However, while the long-term employment potential of high-technology industrial areas has made them the goal of many development agencies seeking growth nodes of high-technology production, the inertia implicit in the agglomeration advantages noted in this chapter suggest that such industries will not be easily enticed from their current areas of concentration.

Appendix 1: Survey MLH and SIC codes with product categories

British Minimum List Headings

Scientific and Industrial instruments and systems: MLH 354

1. Optical instruments Manufacturing lenses, prisms, and other optically worked elements, telescopes, binoculars, monoculars, microscopes, optical surveying instruments, optical metrological instruments, optical density measuring equipment, ophthalmic instruments, photocells and other optical instruments and apparatus. Optical nautical and aeronautical and gunnery control instruments are included, but the grinding of spectacle lenses is classified in Subdivision 2 of MLH 353. Photographic and cinematographic apparatus is classified in MLH 351.

2. Other scientific and industrial instruments and systems Manufacturing scientific instruments, equipment and systems for sensing, measuring, indicating, recording and/or control of mechanical, electrical (including electronic), and magnetic magnitudes, including simple measuring devices such as pressure gauges, meters. Ultrasonic instruments and equipment are included. Mechanical and electrical medical measuring instruments are included, but other electro-medical equipment is classified in MLH 367. Engineers' gauges are classified in MLH 390.

Radio and electronic components: MLH 364

1. Valves and other active components Manufacturing electronic valves (including cathode ray tubes), semi-conductors and electronic rectifiers. Glass envelopes are classified in MLH 463.

2. Integrated circuits Manufacturing thin and thick film passive and hybrid circuits, monolithic semi-conductor circuits. Printed circuits are classified in Subdivision 3 of this heading.

3. Other radio and electronic components Manufacturing resistors, capacitors, inductors, circuit breakers for electronic equipment, sound reproduction components, printed circuits and other components and assemblies not elsewhere specified. The manufacture of electronic components for equipment classified in MLH 365, Subdivision 2 is included. The manufacture of tape decks (other than those for use with computers and related equipment, which is classified in MLH 366) is included.

Equivalent United States Four-digit Standard Industrial Classification codes chosen for the survey

SIC 3800 Instruments and related products

3811 Instruments, engineering and scientific; 3822 Environmental controls; 3823 Instruments, process controls; 3824 Fluid meters and counting devices; 3825 Instruments to measure electricity; 3829 Measuring and control devices (NEC); 3832 Optical instruments and lenses.

SIC 3600 Electric and electronic equipment

3612 Transformers; 3622 Controls, industrial; 3629 Electrical industrial apparatus (NEC); 3671 Electronic tubes, receiving; 3672 Cathode ray TV picture tubes; 3673 Electronic tubes, transmitting; 3674 Semi-conductors and related devices; 3675 Capacitors, electronic; 3676 Resistors, electronic and electric; 3677 Coils and transformers, electronic; 3678 Connectors, electronic; 3679 Electronic components (NEC).

References

Alonso, W. (1971) The Economics of Urban Size. *Papers and proceedings Regional Science Association*, **26**, 67–83.

Bullock, M. (1983) *Academic Enterprise, Industrial Innovation and the Development of High Technology Financing in the United States*. London: Brand Brothers and Co.

Buswell, R. J. and Lewis, E. W. (1970) The geographic distribution of industrial research activity. *Regional Studies*, **4**, pp. 297–306.

Cooper, A. C. (1970) The Palo Alto experience. *Industrial Research*, May, pp. 68–60.

Cross, M. (1981) *New Firm Formation and Regional Development*. Farnborough: Gower.

Deutermann, E. P. (1966) Seeding science based industries. *New England Business Review*, December, pp. 7–15.

Estall, R. C. (1972) Some observations on the internal mobility of investment capital. *Area*, **4**, pp. 193–98.

Feller, J. (1975) Innovation, diffusion and industrial location, in Collins, L. and Walker, D. F. (eds.) *Location Dynamics and Manufacturing Activity*. London: John Wiley.

Freeman, C. (1974) *The Economics of Industrial Innovation*. Harmondsworth: Penguin.

Gibson, J. L. (1970 An analysis of the location of instrument manufacture in the United States, *AAAG*, **60** (2), pp. 352–67.

Gilmour, J. M. (1974) External economies of scale, inter-industrial linkages and decision making in manufacturing, in Hamilton, F. E. I. (ed.) *Spatial Perspectives on Industrial Organisation and Decision Making*. London: John Wiley, pp. 335–63.

Goddard, J. B. (1978) The location of non-manufacturing activities within manufacturing industries, in Hamilton, F. E. I. (ed.) *Contemporary Industrialisation*. London: Longman, pp. 62–85.

Goddard, J. B. and Smith, I. (1978) Changes in corporate control in the British urban system, 1972–77. *Environment and Planning* A, **10**, pp. 1073–84.

Hall, P. G. (1962) *The Industries of London*. London: Hutchinson.

Keeble, D. (1976) *Industrial Location and Planning in the United Kingdom*. London: Methuen.

Kondratieff, N. D. (1935) The long wave in economic life. *Review of Economic Statistics*, **17**, pp. 105–15.

Little, A. D. (1977) *New Technology Based Firms in the United Kingdom and the Federal Republic of Germany*, Report prepared for the Anglo-German Foundation for the Study of Industrial Society.

Luttrell, W. F. (1962) *Factory Location and Industrial Movement*. London: NIESR.

Martin, J. E. (1966) *Greater London: An Industrial Geography*. London: Bell.

Oakey, R. P. (1979*a*), Technological change and regional development: a note on policy implications. *Area*, **11**, pp. 340–4.

Oakey, R. P. (1979*b*) The effect of technical contracts with local research establishments on the location of the British instruments industry. *Area*, **11**, pp. 146–50.

Oakey, R. P. (1981) *High Technology Industry and Industrial Location*. Farnborough: Gower.

Oakey, R. P. (1983) New technology, government policy and regional manufacturing employment. *Area*, **15**, pp. 61–65.

Oakey, R. P. (1984) *High Technology Small Firms: Innovation and Regional Development in British and the United States*. London: Frances Pinter, New York: St Martin's Press.

Oakey, R. P., Thwaites, A. T. and Nash, P. A. (1980) The regional distribution of innovative manufacturing establishments in Britain. *Regional Studies*, **14**, pp. 235–53.

Oakey, R. P., Thwaites, A. T. and Nash, P. A. (1982) Technological change and regional development: some evidence on regional variations in product and process innovation. *Environment and Planning*, A, **14**, pp. 1073–86.

Perroux, F. (1955) Note sur la notion de pôle de croissance. *Economie Appliqué*, **8**, Nos. 1 and 2.

Robertson, A. (1974) Innovation management. *Management Decisions*, **12**, pp. 329–73.

Rothwell, R. and Zegveld, W. (1982) *Innovation and Small and Medium Sized Firm*. London: Frances Pinter.

Smith, D. M. (1970) On throwing Weber out with the bathwater; a note on industrial location and linkage, *Area*, **1**, pp. 15–18.

Smith, I. J. (1979) The effect of external takeovers on manufacturing employment change in the Northern Region between 1963 and 1973. *Regional Studies*, **13**, pp. 421–37.

Storey, D. J. (1982) *Entrepreneurship and the Small Firm*. London: Croom Helm.

Townroe, P. (1971) *Industrial location decisions*, University of Birmingham Centre for Urban and Regional Studies, Occasional Paper No. 15.

Vernon, R. (1966) International investment and international trade in the product cycle. *Quarterly Journal of Economics*, **80**, pp. 190–207.

Weber, A. (1929) *Theory of the Location of Industries*. Chicago: University of Chicago Press.

Wise, M. J. (1951) On the evolution of the gun and jewellery quarters in Birmingham. *Transactions IBG*, **15**, pp. 57–72.

Wood, P. (1969) Industrial location and linkage. *Area*, **2**, pp. 32–9.

Zegveld, W. and Prakke, F. (1978) Government policies and factors influencing the innovative capability of small and medium enterprises, paper presented for the Committee for Scientific and Technological Policy, OECD, Paris.

8

The anatomy of job creation? Industrial change in Britain's M4 Corridor

MICHAEL BREHENY, PAUL CHESHIRE and ROBERT LANGRIDGE

*What is the nature of the growth process
in the M4 Corridor, and what are its causes?
What is the role of high-tech development in
the process and what lessons may be learned
from the experiences of this area?*

A major preoccupation of academics and journalists in Britain in recent years has been the charting of the nation's industrial decline. Very few geographical areas or sectors of the economy have been exempt from this sorry and continuing tale. Given this, it is not surprising that when exceptions are noted, quite a fuss is made. A lot of publicity, particularly in the pages of the property journals, has recently been given to those few parts of the country in which there appears to be a relatively buoyant economy boosted by the development of so-called 'high-tech' industries. The central lowlands of Scotland and Cambridge are two such places, but the area receiving most attention is the 'M4 Corridor' stretching out from west London along the M4 motorway as far as Bristol and even into South Wales. Spread out along this corridor at Maidenhead, Bracknell, Reading, Newbury, Swindon, Bristol and other smaller towns and villages are located, we are told, the majority of Britain's high-tech companies and most of the few 'new' jobs created in the country in recent years.

This area is variously described, in the numerous newspaper and television commentaries that it has spawned, as England's 'Golden West', its 'Sunrise Strip', 'Britain's California within the Home Counties', the area where 'the recession passed almost unnoticed', the 'focus of the next industrial revolution', and Britain's equivalent of California's 'Silicon Valley'. There is a general, if as yet unsubstantiated, feeling that these developments along the M4 may be both a very significant feature of the national economy in their own right, and also a pointer to the future form of the economic geography of Britain and even its spatial settlement pattern.

However, as remarkable as the apparent phenomenon of high-tech growth in the M4 Corridor is our ignorance, in any systematic or rigorous sense, of the precise nature of that growth, of its genesis, of its repercussions, and hence its significance to the national economy now or in the future. Academics in Britain have studiously chronicled the decline of our national, regional and urban manufacturing economies, giving us a substantial understanding of the 'anatomy of job loss' (Massey and Meegan, 1982). What they have not been studying are the limited, but possibly important, instances of job creation. If we are to take the greatest possible advantage of these few glimmers of industrial hope, we need to know what growth has been taking place, we need to know why it has occurred in particular locations at particular times, the factors which sustain it, its likely longevity and a host of possible detailed implications. Only with this knowledge will we know if and how this growth can be replicated, channelled or influenced. If in fact the phenomenon exhibited in the M4 Corridor is much less significant than the press furore would suggest, then better we know sooner rather than later. It would, indeed, be a sick joke to continue to hold out the hope that this development points the way to the nation's, or even the region's, salvation if it is in fact no more than an interesting, but localized and essentially transitory phenomenon. Either way, optimistic or pessimistic, it is obvious that we need to go beyond our current superficial and often anecdotal understanding of events in the M4 Corridor.

This paper attempts to pull together some of this unsatisfactory, but necessary information, and to raise some of the questions that need to be asked as part of a more rigorous study. It also tentatively poses a number of hypotheses about the nature of the growth process in the M4 Corridor that might be tested. As will be explained below, much of the recent relative prosperity of the Corridor is *not* due to high-tech developments at all. For this reason the discussion here is set in a broader context of industrial change in the area generally. However, because the high-tech development is significant and relatively new, and because its genesis is something we do not understand, unlike the parallel and in employment terms more significant office developments, this paper focuses on its contribution to growth along the M4.

Defining High-Tech Industries

Not only does the available literature show an ignorance of the nature of the reasons for the high-tech growth in the M4 Corridor, but it also shows great confusion as to just what constitutes high-technology industry. Such confusion has allowed interested parties the excuse to assign the term 'high tech' to all manner of firms, industries, processes and even building developments. Too often the term 'high tech' is no more than political glibspeak or property developer's advertising copy. Even the few academic or official reports on the M4 Corridor (for example, Berkshire CC, 1982) use the term 'high-tech industries' very vaguely, often referring generally to electronics or electronics-related activities. As we shall see below, producing an adequate definition is not easy, but nevertheless an attempt must be made if we are to have any systematic and common understanding of the issue. It is particularly important that we have a common definition for the purposes of comparing high-tech developments in various parts of Britain or internationally.

Obviously what is required is a definition which is both conceptually and operationally adequate. In both American (Hall and Markusen, 1982) and British work (Langridge, 1983), this has become a priority.

Existing work on defining high-tech industries has tended to follow one of two approaches. The first approach is subjective, with the analyst making a value judgment as to which industries (in Britain usually at the Standard Industrial Classification's Minimum List Heading (MLH) level) warrant classification as high tech. The second approach is more objective, and involves attempts to identify characteristics which, *a priori*, high-technology industries might be expected to exhibit.

The first approach has been used by Oakey (1981), and also in a report to the Standing Conference on London and South-East Regional Planning (1983). Whilst this approach avoids thorny conceptual problems and gives a working definition, it is very unsatisfactory in that it is peculiar to the analysts concerned, has no objective base and makes comparison virtually impossible.

The second approach is more satisfactory because it is based on the idea of deriving a standard, conceptually-sound definition that will enable systematic, comparative work to be carried out. The approach has been investigated by Hall and Markusen (1982, 1983) in the United States. While difficulties have been experienced in obtaining comparable data, both the original criteria adopted in the United States and additional variants have been tested for the United Kingdom (Langridge, 1983).

Initially the Hall-Markusen criteria comprised all industries and services which over a ten-year period had exhibited a 2 per cent per annum growth rate in employment, coupled with a ratio of production workers to total employment 20 per cent below the national average.

This rests on two assumptions: that high-technology industries create higher than average employment opportunities and that occupational composition is of a higher than average professional and technical nature.

They propose to test their model over the period 1967–77, but in view of the apparent time lag between the growth in high-tech firms in the United States and the United Kingdom, the UK tests were conducted over the ten-year period to 1982 (Langridge, 1983).

In the UK tests it was found that only one manufacturing sector MLH, Electronic Computers (366), could meet the Hall-Markusen employment growth criterion. This result was not encouraging, and even after eliminating the recession years 1980–2 from the tests only one further MLH, Radio, Radar and Electronic Capital Goods (367) could be added. On the other hand, in the service sector both Insurance and Banking (XXIV) and Miscellaneous (XXVI) MLHs performed well despite the recession. However, this raised a problem in that, while some high-tech industries may be classified as services, many of the service MLHs, such as Sport and Recreation (882) and Clubs (887) could not intuitively be considered as high tech. In the United States analysis, the second criterion, concerned with the occupational composition of the workforce, would elimate such service sectors. In the United Kingdom, however, the second criterion cannot be applied as the current source of occupational data, the Census of Production, does not cover the service sectors.

Further analysis has been undertaken by Langridge (1983) on the performance of manufacturing MLHs in terms of production output, capital labour ratios, capital output ratios and occupational composition ratios. Analysis of research and development to total sales ratios is to be added in the near future. Nothing conclusive emerged from the capital labour and capital output ratio tests, but more success was achieved by ranking manufacturing MLHs in terms of output growth over the period 1975–80, electronics and chemicals MLHs filling seven out of the top eight positions. Similarly, occupation composition ratios (proxied by operatives to administrative, technical and clerical employees by MLH in 1980) were ranked accordingly. This, however, proved disappointing, with the top ten rankings including Gas, Electricity, Soap, and Printing and Publishing.

The last results are surprising in view of Hall and Markusen's (1983) decision to focus on an occupation composition definition of high-technology industries. There may, however, be significant differences to consider between US and UK data sources and the nature of high-tech industries in the two countries. One difference is that the US studies have been undertaken using comprehensive data for both manufacturing and service sectors. Another is that differences may exist between the nature of high-tech industries in the two countries which could influence the occupational composition of the respective workforces. However, when the UK 1981 Census occupation data became available, some of the tests can be re-run.

In conclusion, we have yet to establish a conceptually and operationally adequate definition of high-tech industry. Nevertheless, detailed analysis of the options is increasing understanding of the difficulties involved, and sustained debate will help to resolve the problem. It may be that one all-embracing, neat definition will be impossible, and that we will have to make do with a set of specific, overlapping definitions used for different purposes. It is significant that some of the American work concerns itself with each of a series of high-tech sectors (see Markusen on software, robotics, biotechnology and photovoltaics in this book), which are relatively easily defined, rather than with comprehensive assessments of high-tech industries.

Structural Adaptation in Berkshire

The M4 Corridor's comparative success is not because it has been exempt from the forces of decline so evident elsewhere in Britain. Swindon, for example, was built as a railway town, but that source of employment has declined, as it has in other centres. Although the information is comparatively fragmentary, more is known of Reading and West Berkshire (Newbury); areas we may look at as examples of structural adaptation in the economy of the M4 Corridor.

Reading was as good a copy of a northern nineteenth-century industrial town as could be found in the south of England. Its growth stemmed from its role as a prosperous agricultural and transport centre. Its industrial employment was based on 'beer, biscuits and bulbs'. Of these industrial or quasi-industrial activities only beer remains, and even here there has been a characteristic closure/relocation process. The old Courage brewery in the town centre has closed, and production has been relocated in a highly capital-intensive new plant beside the M4. The transfer involved the loss of 300 jobs in Reading and more in London, since it coincided with the closure of the company's Southwark site. Suttons Seeds left Reading for Devonshire, with the loss of a further 300 jobs, in 1976, and Huntley and Palmers closed their manufacturing activities in the town in 1977. At its early twentieth-century peak, this factory had provided 8000 jobs, though at the time of closure there were only 1100 remaining. Other, older manufacturing plants have closed or contracted, including the rainwear makers Burberrys and the Gillette plant.

For statistical purposes, since the urban area of Reading spreads far beyond its administrative boundaries, probably the closest approximation to it is Central Berkshire. Table 8.1 summarizes the available evidence on employment changes in both Central and West Berkshire, two key districts at the heart of what is now thought of as the M4 Corridor, between 1966 and 1977. Unfortunately, the 1981 Census results are not yet available for comparable area/sector breakdown.

Table 8.1   Employment (in thousands) and percentage change in employment.

| | Central Berks | | | West Berks* | | | |
	1966	1971	1977	1966	1971	1971	1977
Primary	2.9	2.3	1.6	1.5	1.6	1.4	1.4
% Change		−20.7	−30.4		+6.7		0
Manufacturing	34.0	38.6	34.5	6.1	6.5	5.9	6.2
% Change		+13.5	−10.6		+6.6		+5.1
Construction	12.1	10.7	11.9	2.1	2.8	1.7	1.5
% Change		+11.6	+11.2		+33.3		−11.8
Public utilities and transport	10.4	10.8	9.7	2.1	2.2	2.2	1.8
% Change		+3.8	−10.2		+4.8		−18.2
Business and professional services and administration	38.5	44.2	57.2	5.9	5.9	5.9	7.6
% Change		+14.8	+29.4		0.0		+28.8
Distribution and miscellaneous services	33.7	33.2	43.8	7.9	7.8	5.4	8.0
% Change		−1.5	+31.9		−1.3		+48.1
Total†	131.6	139.8	158.7	25.8	27.0	22.5	26.4
% Change		+6.2	+13.5		+4.7		+17.3

* Census of Population & Census of Employment are not strictly comparable.
† Includes some unclassified.
Sources: 1966 and 1971 Census: 1971 (West Berkshire) and 1977 Census of employment.

However, the survey of employment carried out by Berkshire County Council in 1981 shows that between 1977 and 1981 in the firms surveyed, the employment changes were as shown in table 8.2.

Thus if we assume that most high-tech employment is in manufacturing, it seems implausible to believe that this category has made the major contribution to the prosperity of the Central and West Berkshire

Table 8.2   Employment change 1977–81.

	Central Berks	West Berks
Manufacturing	−2,200	−800
Non-manufacturing	+2,100	−100
Total	− 100	−900

Note: These area definitions are not strictly comparable with those in table 8.1.

sectors of the M4 Corridor. The major contribution has in fact been made by office development, in the process of office decentralization analysed briefly below. Employment in the main office sectors, Business and Professional Services and Public Administration grew by 13,000 in Central Berkshire alone in the period 1971–7, generating a small and unusual growth in the construction sector.

Further evidence of office employment is produced by figures on office development. Applying the office space per employee figures derived from the Berkshire CC employment survey (1982) to the amount of office space completed in the period 1976–81, produces a (gross) job creation of 7150 in Central Berkshire and 550 in West Berkshire; developments in the pipeline in 1981 implied a further gross increment of 12,000 office jobs in Central Berkshire, with a much sharper relative increase in West Berkshire. Despite the fact that these figures appear to the authors to be somewhat high, they demonstrate the substantial role of new office development in explaining recent employment changes in this part of the M4 Corridor.

Elucidating the precise role of high-tech firms in the comparative success of the local economy is more difficult. Probably the most reliable source of information is the report of the Berkshire CC employment survey (1982) already referred to. The definition of 'high tech' used was subjective, and included firms in both the manufacturing (for example, electronics) and service sectors (for example, software). The survey found that employment in high-tech firms present in both 1977 and 1981 had grown by 10 per cent compared to a reduction of 6 per cent in employment in all 'established' employers as a group. Another indicator was that of high-tech firms, 57 per cent were new, in the sense that they had not existed in 1977, compared to 27 per cent of total employers; 12 per cent of all new firms were high tech, compared to 4 per cent of established firms. In total, employment in high-tech firms in the survey accounted for 12 per cent of that in the private sector, and an estimated 20,000 in the whole of Berkshire.

From these data, although no final conclusions can be drawn, it is clear that the more extravagant claims of the proponents of high tech are, at least to date, not warranted by the evidence. The growth of this sector has been a significant factor in the success of Berkshire's economy, and the signs are that it will be more significant in the future. But in terms of its direct contribution to employment, the sector has provided far less than the growth of offices. However, as is discussed in the next section, this office growth itself owes much to the application of high technology.

Office Employment Decentralization

Since the single most important direct source of employment growth along the M4, and certainly in Berkshire, has been office growth, a brief analysis of that phenomenon is appropriate. This is particularly true since most of the office growth results from decentralization, which in turn is largely due to the application of the very kinds of high technology being produced in the area.

The reasons for the success of the large central office block were, and are, economic. These blocks provided the cheapest way of fulfilling a certain function. In a large organization there are strong, sometimes critical, advantages for key decision-makers being located at the heart of a large urban area. The elite decision-makers of a major bank, insurance company or manufacturing concern, depend crucially on a constant flow of information and face-to-face contact. This contact will be with their immediate supporting staff, with the elites of other organizations with whom they do business or on whom they depend for services, and with government. The cheapest way of achieving this was in a single large office block or perhaps a set of offices close to each other in the heart of London or of other major cities. There were other minor advantages to such an arrangement, such as the prestige of a central London address and perhaps a preference, particularly by the elite, for living and operating in London.

These factors have been changing for some time now, however, and, coinciding with the changes, has been a period of extreme pressure on companies' financial resources making them look more closely than ever at their cost structures.

The most important underlying change that has occurred might be described as a specialized transport cost. The application of high technology in offices has produced a revolution in data processing, storage, retrieval and communication. The potential of this is to cut to a small fraction of its original level the penalty cost of separating the elite decision-makers and their general staffs from their routine back-up employees. Further, it reduces the need, and so the cost advantage, of continual direct face-to-face communication with other decision-making elites. Coupled with the significant savings in rents and labour costs which, because the new technology demands more space per employee, become more critical, this implies a decentralization of office employment to either suburban centres or increasingly to functionally-integrated satellite centres such as Reading. There, both rents and labour are significantly cheaper than in central locations.

This has been one of the prototypal moves of the past ten years; the splitting of office employment into two groups; one group of employees engaged in routine work using high technology and generating a rapid expansion of demand for up-to-date and quite large-scale office space away from the traditional centres; another and typically much smaller, unit remaining in a central location in a luxury suite. The directors' penthouse suite may have grown; it may have stayed in or even moved to the City; but the records register will have been moved to Reading or places similar.

There may increasingly be another sort of move also; a wholesale relocation of complete units, leaving little more than an accommodation address in central London (or central wherever). This may be expected to occur among those firms whose decision-making elites derive least advantage from central locations. In Reading these moves are already apparent with the arrival of Metal Box; in Newbury Bayer will soon be established. Such firms may in some cases be relatively self-contained and interact as much with suppliers in, say, the Midlands or abroad as with bankers in the City or public relations firms in the West End. More interestingly a young growing finance firm, Avco, has now established itself in Reading.

As decentralization proceeds, it becomes cumulative. The new decentralized locations themselves have attracted firms concerned in providing specialized back-up services – for example, financial, legal, public relations, catering or conference facilities – and so the relative advantage of central locations falls further and results in yet more firms moving out. These ancillary firms themselves generate a demand for small but high-quality premises and the new decentralized sub-centres.

Explaining the High-Tech Phenomenon

It is important, then, in assessing high-tech developments along the M4, to appreciate this context of general structural adaptation and particularly of office decentralization. But having set this context, what are the questions that need to be asked if we are to gain the more rigorous understanding of these high-tech activities urged earlier? It is suggested here that these questions can usefully be posed in two groups; firstly, there are the fundamental issues of the nature and genesis of the high-tech developments along the M4; secondly, there is a series of questions concerning specific features and implications of this type of growth, including policy issues.

The Genesis of Growth

The available, journalistic literature on the M4 Corridor discusses the reasons for the recent high-tech developments in terms of the locational advantages of the area, and tends to look for relatively simple contemporary causes. There is little doubt that these locational advantages have been significant. The area does have excellent communications, with a good motorway network focused on the M4 itself, a high-speed rail service and ready access to Heathrow, the largest international airport in the world. It also has an attractive physical environment, which appears to be an important factor in attracting highly-skilled, discriminating staff, and also, now, a highly-skilled workforce.

It is likely, however, that a sound explanation of the genesis of growth in the M4 Corridor will be more complex than these accounts would suggest. It is possible that these locational advantages can explain the continued growth in the area. It is not difficult to see that once established in the Corridor, growth has gained its own momentum due to these locational advantages, plus the benefits of increasing agglomeration economies. The locational advantages, however, may not be sufficient to explain why high-tech industry began in the area in the first place. This may require a more detailed historical analysis.

Before proposing hypotheses to explain this genesis, it is important to point out one further general determining factor. The growth of high-tech development in the M4 Corridor is consistent with, and must be partly attributable to, general changes in the British space economy. During the post-war period we have seen a consistent pattern of decentralization, most recently of offices, with a neat inverse relationship between rates of population and employment change and the size of urban areas (Fothergill and Gudgin, 1981; Berg *et al.*, 1981). It is precisely the smaller free-standing towns like Reading, Swindon, or Newbury, and their smaller satellites in turn, that one would expect to have been prospering relatively, even without the added impetus of high tech. This effect, plus its additional communication and environmental advantages, meant that the M4 Corridor was always in a strong position to take advantage of any industrial opportunities that came along.

Given this general context of relative locational advantage, and the impetus given to growth by the office decentralization mentioned earlier, we can now begin to posit hypotheses as to the genesis of high-tech growth specifically. These hypotheses are not mutually exclusive, and are intended simply as a means of systematically assessing the causes of growth.

The first hypothesis is that of *indigenous technological growth*. This suggests that the seeds of the M4 technological developments and their subsequent growth were of British origin. It is generally acknowledged that the piecemeal location of government research establishments in the area after the war has something to do with the initial, earliest developments and with subsequent changes. Certainly these research centres are thick on the ground; for example there is atomic energy research at Aldermaston and Harwell, aircraft research at Farnborough and Bristol and transportation research at Bracknell. As they grew after the war, more and more highly educated and skilled staff were recruited to work within them. In addition, skilled and specialized sub-contractors in engineering, electrical engineering and electronics developed to serve the needs of the research establishments.

It seems likely that in the late 1960s and early 1970s a number of developments occurred around these research centres, their staff and their supporting services. Firstly, it is suggested that the more entrepreneurially-minded scientists and technicians came to appreciate that much of their work had potential commercial application. Although the individual projects they were working on were classified, the scientific processes and information technologies they were using were not; and they had wide applicability. Consequently, individuals began to leave the government research centres and set up their own companies to produce, for instance, electronic hardware and computer software. Thus pure research concepts, originating in publically-financed research establishments, came to be developed in private commercial firms as part of an indigenous technological development process. This is close but not identical to the model developed by Saxenian (1981) for Silicon Valley (see also chapter 2).

As a second development, in addition to this process of public employees becoming high-tech private entrepreneurs, it is likely that the presence of the government scientists and researchers also attracted small immigrant high-tech firms anxious to recruit from amongst the ranks of the research establishments. In either case, whether the initial firms were spawned directly by the research centre staff or were small immigrants attracted by them, it is likely that further staff would continue to be recruited from the research centres.

A third possible element in this hypothesis is that much of the growth originates from those sub-contractors mentioned earlier, who originally located in the area to support the research establishments. On the back of government contracts these firms may have gradually expanded their operations from being local support services to high-tech exporters. They were in the ideal position, of course, both to benefit from any government research spin-off and to recruit from the research centres.

The likelihood, of course, is that all three of these processes were in operation at the same time and account in some way for the establishment of high-tech industry along the M4. This hypothesis maintains that whatever the specific contribution of these processes, the driving force behind the phenomenon is indigenous scientific and technological know-how and endeavour.

The second hypothesis states that we are dealing in the M4 Corridor with *imported technology growth*. Far from being a result of native genius and enterprise, events along the M4 owe as much to the National Aeronautical Space Administration in the United States as to the Ministry of Defence. According to this view, the major activity of the largest firms in the area is not so much Research and Development as component sub-assembly, warehousing and distribution. In other words, the M4 acts for these firms as Heathrow's longest runway, providing an easy access into Europe in two senses. First, Britain's common language and, later, membership of the EEC meant that American firms based here could avoid language and associated problems and avoid customs tariffs and delays, into the British market and later into Europe too. Secondly, given the proximity of the Corridor to Heathrow, the movement of key personnel and cargo into Western Europe was a relatively easy matter. Slightly later, especially following accession to the EEC, US multinationals were joined by Japanese ones. In this view, the relationship of the major firms to indigenous public research facilities is largely coincidental.

A third possible hypothesis is a more complex one, consisting of a *hybrid of indigenous and imported determinants* of growth. This argues that whilst the origin of high-technology industry in the Corridor was originally mainly as a result of foreign multinationals such as Digital finding it a convenient location from which to penetrate the British and European markets, there was at a subsequent stage a change of causal mechanism. The presence of specialized labour and skills in the research establishments and defence industries when blended with the skills and resources of the incoming multinationals produced a large enough pool of interacting skills and demands for a genuine fusion to take place. At some stage, therefore, perhaps in the mid-1970s, sufficient agglomeration had occurred for internal and indigenous growth processes to take off. In as far as an explanation such as this proved to be true, then it would provide important insights into both the nature of agglomeration economies in these activities and the extent of their 'footlooseness'. The Berkshire CC finding that 57 per cent of all high-tech firms observed in 1981 had been established since 1977 perhaps lends some support to this hypothesis.

Clearly, testing these hypotheses on the genesis of growth in the M4 Corridor requires a careful and detailed historical analysis, aimed not at describing change but at explaining it. It would seem that, as in the case of studies of Silicon Valley, this has to be done by tracking the early role of particular companies and even individuals. A company genealogy, as produced for Silicon Valley, would help on this. If hypothesis two has any credence, then this detailed, localized analysis has to be supplemented by a much broader assessment of the activities of the multinationals in the world high-tech economy.

Issues and Implications

A full explanation of the genesis of growth in the M4 Corridor should open up possibilities for investigating a series or more detailed aspects of this kind of industrial development and allow some of its broader implications to be assessed.

One particular aspect of concentrated high-technology growth of interest to researchers is that of *agglomeration economies*. If these can be identified, then policies to assist their development, both along the M4 and elsewhere, could be investigated. If on the other hand they are found to be weak, this would imply that such industries are 'foot-loose', with equally important policy implications. It may be that these agglomeration economies are different for different types of high-tech companies.

Another important aspect of high-technology growth concerns the nature of the *labour markets* created. High-technology industry almost certainly has specialized demands for labour. We need to know whether the skills that are required represent a constraint on employment growth; with obvious implications for manpower and training policies, and for movements of labour either by way of commuting or of permanent migration. There is some evidence (see chapter 3) that high-technology industry has some unusual labour market effects. It tends, for instance, to produce what Markusen (see page 39) terms a 'highly bifurcated occupational structure', or what has been called elsewhere a 'polarized workforce'. This is the situation in which the workforce is composed of a small elite of highly-skilled, highly-paid, mobile engineers and scientists on the one hand, and the rest of the semi-skilled workforce on the other. The former group will be almost entirely male and the latter group increasingly female dominated. These labour market effects are likely to be very different in specific high-tech sectors. Perhaps the most important labour market issue concerns the overall employment generation effects of high-tech industry. Using American evidence again, we would be unwise to assume that large numbers of jobs are going to be created. Certainly high-tech jobs will not compensate for the job losses in traditional declining industries, even in areas like the M4 Corridor. In America the suggestion is (see page 39) that they do not even compensate for the job losses due to the introduction of the new technologies that they themselves are based on (see chapters 3 and 6). Clearly, investigation of these labour market issues is crucial, as the chapter by Weiss demonstrates.

Clearly the growth of high-technology industry will have a profound effect both on *local and national economies*. This can, however, only be understood in the light of knowledge of development and growth processes and of internal and external economies and diseconomies of scale. If the location factors prove to imply small average scale and rapid development of·external diseconomies of agglomeration, there would be one set of implications; if the reverse, a quite different set of conclusions would obtain. Similarly we should want to understand the extent of indirect local income and employment generation. Also, it is important to understand the links that may exist between high-technology industry in an area like Berkshire with the wider national economy, whether in producer-good or consumer-good industries.

It has been suggested in the United States that high-tech industries, just because they depend on new forms of agglomeration economies, have fewer internal economies of scale than traditional manufacturing; they depend on new forms of communication and are influenced strongly in their location by environmental factors. Therefore, it is argued, they will tend to engender *new forms of urbanization*, probably in areas that previously were not urbanized. There is nothing in the M4 Corridor phenomenon to contradict this view. However, there are other forces obviously producing the same effects, and it will be difficult to determine the role played by the location decisions of high-tech firms within a general decentralization process. As the discussion of office development earlier suggested, the products of the high-tech firms, particularly the new information technologies, may be having a much more profound effect on urbanization patterns than the decisions of the firms themselves.

A major and obvious issue that arises from all of this is that of *policy intervention*. The question at all scales, from the national to the regional to the local, is to what extent is it possible to develop successful policy intervention to influence and/or control the development and location of new high-tech activities. Nationally, the question must be part of any attempt to resurrect regional policy. At the regional scale, the obvious but unplanned concentration of the high-tech benefits in a few areas gives yet one more reason for a new phase of vigorous intra-regional planning. Nowhere is the need for this more obvious than in the south-east of England. At the local scale there are numerous issues. In Berkshire, for example, there is a significant body of local opinion opposed to further development, including high-tech initiatives. Central government is inclined to encourage new industrial development wherever it wants to go. Here then, is an issue that combines national and local interests. It may prove to be significant that areas that may on the face of it be attractive to high-tech firms, such as Hertfordshire, may not want them. Another local problem concerns the suggestion that high-technology activities fail to conform to existing land-use planning classifications and practices, so that planners find it difficult to repond to them, with the result that their development is inhibited. This view is challenged by the local planning authorities, but clearly needs investigation.

Conclusion

Despite our ignorance of its origins, its implications and its ultimate significance, there is no doubt that something is happening along the M4 Corridor and that it is in part due to high-tech industries. It gains in significance because it currently goes against the national, depressing, downhill grain. In principle, it has profound implications for national and local economies, for a host of employment and labour market issues and for possible policy and planning initiatives. Recent change in the Corridor is not just a figment of the collective mind of enthusiastic property agents, even if they have done a good job of 'hyping' it. But whether it really is the 'focus of the next industrial revolution' is doubtful. One thing is sure, however. These changes, associated in large part with new high-technology companies, are sufficiently significant that we need to make absolutely certain that we are doing our best to understand them. We cannot afford to remain ignorant of something that *may* point the way to a more prosperous industrial future.

References

Berg, L. v.d., Drewett, R. Klaassen, L., Rossi, A. and Vijverberg, C. (1981) *Urban Europe, Vol. 1, A Study of Urban Growth and Decline*. Oxford: Pergamon.

Berkshire County Planning Department (1982) *Report of the 1981 Survey of Employers*. Reading: Berkshire County Council.

Fothergill, S. and Gudgin, G. (1982) *Unequal Growth*. London: Heinemann Educational Books.

Hall, P. and Markusen, A. (1982) *Innovation and Regional Growth*, proposal to the National Science Foundation. Institute of Urban and Regional Development, University of California, Berkeley (unpublished).

Langridge, R. (1983) *Defining High Technology Industries*. Department of Economics Working Paper, University of Reading (forthcoming).

Massey, D. and Meegan, R. (1982) *The Anatomy of Job Loss. The How, Why and Where of Employment Decline*. London: Methuen.

Oakey, R. (1982) *High Technology Industry and Industrial Location*. Aldershot: Gower.

Saxenian, A. (1981) *Silicon Chips and Spatial Structure*. Institute of Urban and Regional Development Working Paper No. 335, University of Califonia, Berkeley.

Standing Conference on London and South-East Regional Planning (1983) *South East Regional Monitor SC1812*. London: Standing Conference.

Acknowledgement

Many of the points made in this paper have arisen during group discussions at the University of Reading. Peter Hall, Doug Hart and Paschal Preston have been involved in these discussions, and their help is gratefully acknowledged.

9

High-technology industry and the development of science parks

TONY TAYLOR

If high-technology development,
and science parks in particular, are to
be successful in the United Kingdom, better
planning at all levels is needed.

As long ago as 1968 Melvin Webber quoted Brzezinski as saying that society was entering a metamorphic phase in human history, a phase so revolutionary in nature that viewed from the long perspective it would make the French and Russian Revolutions seem like 'scratches on the surface of the human condition'. Robespierre and Lenin are indeed mild reformers compared to the microchip! Brzezinski's prophesy suggested the advent of a new Kondratieff cycle, where a sequence of innovations precipitates an industrial revolution, with economic decline and pessimism displaced by technological rejuvenation and an age of optimism.

Even the late 1960s, when Webber was writing, was a period of growth and confident expectations of increasing Western affluence on an unprecedented scale, so there seemed more complacency than warning in Brzezinski's words; complacency that the future would take care of us, that non-employment as opposed to unemployment would relieve Western man from the burden of the misguided Calvinistic work ethic, and that creative leisure would become the norm. There was no thought of world recession, of spiralling inflation, of mass unemployment, or of the rapid industrial decline of the secondary sector currently being experienced. Perhaps this state of affairs could and should have been anticipated. Futurologists could have predicted it even working on the flimsy subjective basis of historic precedent. Bertrand Russell in *The Scientific Outlook*, published in 1931, argued that the universe and human history is 'all spots and jumps'. At each historic turning point, mankind is confronted by the fortuitous and the unforeseen. At such times the ordinary arguments of causality are by no means sufficient in themselves to explain the next stage of the story, the next turn of events.

Whether societal and economic transfiguration is genuinely taking place, or whether the Western world is experiencing a straightforward traditional hiatus in its economic order, is a matter of debate. What is not in doubt, however, are the symptoms of panic which are being engendered; symptoms endemic, for instance, in the present scramble by local authorities, by quasi-public agencies and by the private sector to make a Disraelian leap in the dark for the science and technological shore. Indeed, those parts of the United Kingdom most affected by massive economic decline (inevitably the older industrial cities) are attempting to precipitate Brzezinski's revolution by clutching at high technology, more particularly science and technological parks, as their sole panacea for future survival. They have not the time, it appears, for calm appraisal, for wider options. Votes and jobs are needed *now*. The point is lost that without the support of a genuine regional and economic planning framework they have no future. The market is working too strongly against them.

The age of the old industrial city could well be over. The only surprise is that realization of this comes as a surprise, for, in fact, the decline of the secondary industrial sector is no unexpected event, no less foreseeable than the shift which took place in the nineteenth century from an agricultural-based to an industrial capitalist-based society. The location and form of most British manufacturing industry is the consequence of the social and technological changes of the social and technological changes which were unleashed 150 years ago. Present day social and technological changes are having an equally dramatic effect upon the locational and structural determinants of industrial formation, indeed upon its very *raison d'être*. In addition to the decline in the older industrial cities, there has been a commensurate reversal in the fortunes of those second generation industrial cities, recently so affluent and based originally upon light engineering, because of increasing competition elsewhere in the world. This competition has come particularly from the newly-emerging industrial economies of the Far East and the Third World. Twin factors in the decline of employment in the secondary sector, therefore, can be crudely identified as the competitiveness of world producers and the advance of technology which allows surviving industry to operate with a much reduced workforce. But again, why should this come as a surprise? Does not the situation invite new responses to its challenge?

There is no clear definition of what is embraced by the term high-technology development although some attempts have been made. It has two distinct aims, viz *information technology*, the knowledge-based industries which rely upon the application of knowledge to the invention and assembly of an enlarging range of diverse products, and *biotechnology* based upon energy processes for pharmaceutical, chemical innovation, the development of new materials, and for genetic engineering. Saxon (1982) asserts that there is 'an enormous range of actual and potential activities covered by the information and biological technologies and they are subject to very rapid change as their technologies develop'.

Science and technological parks offer merely one response amongst many to the new economic demands. It is vital for the British economy that the new technologies be developed and applied, and for their physical needs to be translated into development initiatives in whatever form. It has to be emphasized, however, that science and technological parks, however defined, are only one of several ways in which technology can be encouraged. This point is fundamental. Within any national or regional economic policy, therefore, it is important that science and technological park developments are seen in the context of, and alongside other high-technology development initiatives. The locational preferences of science park developers, and the high-technology industries they seek to attract, may well be at variance with carefully prepared structure plan and regional policies. This chapter will show that this is usually the case at the present time when market orientation is extremely strong. These preferences may prove acceptable within a regional plan, indeed they could form the basis of regional economic growth in some areas, whilst other development initiatives may be appropriate elsewhere. But science and technology parks are by no means the universal panacea for economic recovery. The instinctive reaction of some local authorities to grasp for them as straws may be, to an extent, understandable, but in terms of local, regional and national economic policy may prove to be ill-considered.

What are the locational requirements which distinguish science parks from other forms of industrial development? What are the intrinsic characteristics which make them appropriate for some city-regions and not for others? Not surprisingly the well-established economic factor of communications is still the most important requirement with the emphasis, however, on the motorway system and the proximity of a major international airport rather than on canal and rail which was the case in the first Industrial Revolution. Allied to these attributes is the advantage offered by a high-quality natural as well as a social environment, the latter characteristic including the presence of established, proven universities, tertiary education establishments, research institutions and a highly-skilled labour force. Middle-sized, rather than large, towns or cities offer the highest potential because of their scale, the availability of greenfield suburban sites in high-amenity locations, and access to the necessary social infrastructure such as good quality residential areas, schools and public facilities. These factors in combination point to towns like Cambridge, Oxford, Reading, Swindon and Guildford as offering the greatest potential. However, all future high-technology developments need not require all these locational and spatial advantages. Every new development will not necessarily be sited in greenfield locales or in new wave, more prestigious, image-conscious buildings. In some cases the greatest importance will certainly be attached to the links with established universities or research institutions. In other cases, priority will be given to straightforward commercial property investment requirements. Because theory and practice diverge in several basic ways, it has proved difficult to agree upon a common definition of high-technology development. This is not important in itself, in so far as the market is concerned, but it does create problems for planners and local government policy-makers seeking to prepare statements of local economic policy.

What types of development, therefore, are implied as being apposite for establishment within a science and technological park and how did the term itself originate? Its origins have been consistently identified in the United States, where its embryo evolved through the university links at Stanford, California and MIT, Massachusetts. The essential link between high technology and universities was first officially recognized in Britain by the famous Harold Wilson letter of 1966 to all universities in the country in which he exhorted them to develop their own science parks and thus encourage the growth of high-technology concerns. It is conjectural whether this Wilson initiative owed anything to the already established American experiences at Stanford or MIT. It may have been a spontaneous reaction in the euphoria of election victory. Although the Labour administration of the mid-1960s was an age of much rhetoric, 'the forging of the white hot technological revolution', 'the dynamic 100 days', etc., it was as direct response to the Wilson letter that the seeds of the Cambridge and Heriot Watt Science Parks were sown; Trinity College, Cambridge, with its heritage of scientific performance, actively promoting the first.

In essence, the concept of the science and technological park evokes images of attractive natural and designed landscapes, high-quality building design, low-density site coverage and a highly-skilled labour force. The image is not always an accurate reflection of reality and certainly the American fore-runner was much more prosaic in style and setting. Parts of Silicon Valley even today are of little visual quality. The failure rate of science parks in the United States has been high, failures including some sites of extremely high environmental quality. A salient reason for failure often has been the 'pseudo' nature of the development; that is to say they have often been purely commercially speculative in character, presented with a glossy marketing image in the hope of attracting any sort of 'modern' industry whatsoever. Such presentation is usually made in haste in order to be 'first in', but not based upon a proper perception of the supporting elements essential for success; that is the absence of a qualified, skilled labour force, of potential tenants, of the necessary ancillary infrastructure, of high-order transportation networks, and of the presence of too many alternative competing outlets in the area. The failure rate in the United States has shown that a vital ingredient for a successful science park is the participation of a university which has an existing relationship between industry and its own science, mathematics or engineering departments, a relationship which is, at the same time, supportive of research and development initiatives.

This review has, thus far, tended to concern itself with science and technological parks as opposed to high-technology development in general. In attempting to make such a review, however, it is initially necessary to prepare some classification of the many high-technology forms which exist in order that the place of science parks within the wider spectrum can be clearly distinguished.

A science park has been defined by Worthington (1982) as

> operationally, a grouping of research organizations and businesses devoted to the development of scientifically proven concepts from the laboratory stage to the commercial factory production stage; physically, a group of small to medium sized office and laboratory type structures in a high quality landscaped setting; locationally, sited in close relationship with one or more universities, polytechnics or research institutions.

Few science parks possess all these attributes, many being purely commercial speculations and only a handful having genuine university or polytechnic links. Although many universities in Britain are showing an interest in the concept, and the number of proposals grows monthly, at the last count only twelve tertiary education institutions were actively sponsoring their own parks. Of these a mere three, Cambridge, Heriot Watt and Aston, have made substantial progress.

Worthington (1982) identified five types of high-technology development centres.

1   Innovation Centres, within or alongside a university campus, which provide small units for firms growing out of research or expertise within the university. They are usually housed in existing build-

ings. These are the research environments described by Hall and Markusen (1982) as not ones of primary invention, but 'rather the development of invention into a commercially utilizable product'. These writers also argue that an innovation can also consist in product packaging and marketing rather than in a new product per se. Examples of such innovation centres exist in Britain at Lancaster (Enterprise Lancaster), Hull, and Liverpool (Merseyside Innovation Centre). They are all housed in converted warehouse buildings, far from the accepted image of a science park in a sylvan setting. Interestingly, it is in centres such as these that the early Stanford innovations were housed, the genesis of the present Silicon Valley.

2 *Science and Research Parks* are developments designed for growing or established firms in research and development which can be associated with university research laboratories and ancillary amenities. They have workshop, laboratory and office functions. Within Worthington's classification they should be joint ventures between the private sector and a tertiary education establishment, although they do not necessarily need to be sponsored or funded by the latter organizations. Examples of this kind or development include those so far described at Trinity (Cambridge), Heriot Watt (Edinburgh), Aston (Birmingham) as well as more recent ones at the University of Warwick, the West of Scotland (Glasgow) and Salford.

3 *Technology Parks* comprise establishments which undertake a high proportion of applied research, possibly but not essentially involving a university. To be successful they require high-quality housing in the immediate vicinity and university and research institutions within a 30-mile radius. The character of the physical and social environment is an important prerequisite in order to attract scientific and professional staff. These developments are invariably carried out at a low building density in landscaped settings. British examples include the progenitor Birchwood (Warrington), as well as Kirkton (Livingston), Lynch Wood (Peterborough) and Listerhills (Bradford).

4 *Commercial/Business Parks*, involve high-quality, low-density environments with accommodation intended for commercial firms requiring a prestigious image and a high-calibre workforce. They do not require a link with an academic institution but need to be essentially attractive to a mixture of manufacturing, sales, support and professional service functions. The most notable example of this form of park is Aztec West (Bristol). There are others at Linford Wood (Milton Keynes), Kembray Park (Swindon) and Killingworth (Tyne and Wear).

5   *Upgraded Industrial Estates*. There are a great number of straightforward industrial estate developments which have been caught up
in the science park image and are presented and marketed as such.
Whereas they have little or no direct connection with high tech,
their quality of design and appearance has benefited as a consequence of the visual standards being set by the genuine high-
tech schemes. In architectural and landscaping terms they are a
vast improvement on the stereotyped developments of the 1950s
and 1960s. Good examples of these schemes include the Sutton
Industrial Estate (Reading), Southfields (Basildon), Witton (Birmingham) and McKay Trading Estate (London).

Definitions and distinctions apart, it is obvious that there is no limit
at the present time in terms of the number of sites being developed
under the generic high-technology umbrella. However, the market for
a fairly, as yet, restricted field in Britain is bound to become
increasingly competitive. Inevitably, to survive and thrive each
further addition to the field, as well as those existing, will need to
identify clearly its objectives and the sector of the market at which it is
aiming. Segal (1982) has outlined three major objectives in this
respect:

(i)   the encouragement of technology transfer and the linking of
      university resources to tenant companies' development;
(ii) the stimulation of new technology enterprises and structures;
      and
(iii) the attraction of mobile research and development projects of
      large companies.

The significance of the high-technology phenomenon lies perhaps
not so much in semantic debate over what precisely is a science park
and other categorizations, or in the commercial and municipal
scramble to get a high-technology share at all costs, but rather in its
stop-go character, which makes future demand uncertain and the
failure rate of ill-conceived or poorly-sited developments high. The
market is inevitably cautious over long-term prospects where revolutionary or even innovatory change is being undertaken. In the short
term too, there is a limit to the number of sites required; the benefits
take a long time to materialize. Where centres of innovation should
ideally be located is equally unpredictable. Criteria revolving around
the clear attributes of road and air accessibility coupled with presence
of a university and high-quality environment, as already discussed,
are obvious locational starters. Analysis based purely on these
attributes, however, is simplistic and could prove misleading. Recent

research suggests that the innovatory capacity of various regions differs materially. UK studies indicate that South East England has displayed a greater innovative capacity than other areas of the country. Hall and Markusen (1982) argue that new industry will be a spin-off from fundamental university research, and that increasingly new high-technology industry will develop 'around old established and prestigious universities'. This point about the necessity of university-industry linkages is continually stressed. It was first firmly made forty years ago by the late Professor F. E. Terman, then of Stanford University, who emphasized that universities are more than places for learning. 'They are', he said, 'major economic influences in the nation's industrial life, affecting the location of industry, population groups and the character of communities. Universities are a natural resource.' It was as a result of Terman's initiative that cooperation between Stanford and sections of American industry at personal and at collective levels was instigated. He supported the establishment of business and research companies by students, offering encouragement and advice. Two such students were Messrs Hewlett and Packard who today are Hewlett-Packard, the multi-billion dollar corporation. The germ of the present Silicon Valley complex was planted nearly forty years ago as a consequence of the exhortations of Terman and others (see chapter 2). The principle of academic-industrial cooperation still remains, the strongest basis for ultimate success, an essential element when viewed in the global dynamic terms of the Kondratieff cycle, a vital stage in intellectual and technological progress.

High-technology development in Britain today, as has been shown, is in its relative infancy compared to the United States and even to other Western European states. Its future course will undoubtedly be erratic. The forging of true academic-industrial links is vital. So is its correct location, although this may be more difficult to identify for there is a certain ambivalence about locational attraction, despite the obvious qualities of some areas over others. There *are* powerful locational factors but they are not the only ones to be taken into account when considering the initial decision to invest either in a science park or in any other form of high-tech development. Funding, for instance, will be a salient determinant in this regard; a major influence in any development appraisal. At the present time the funding of high-tech schemes, particularly those directly involving a tertiary educational establishment, is a decidedly difficult matter. There is no single source of finance, no one large central pot out of which aid can be supplied. Analysis of the grant assistance available for the establishment of Britain's most significant science parks, for example, indicates an extremely fragmented pattern. Aston has access to venture funds, Heriot Watt to Scottish Development Agency support, Bradford to intermediate development area assistance plus local authority aid, Hull to Inner City Grants and Manpower Services Commission schemes funding, Liverpool and Glasgow to Special Development Area funds as well as local authority aid, Salford to Enterprise Zone and Inner Urban Area Act 1978 incentives, and Warwick to local authority assistance by both the district and county councils for the area.

However, whilst government financial aid appears to be *ad hoc*, and that of the private funding sector distinctly limited, it is implicitly part of the government's industrial policy to promote industrial competitiveness and high-technology development through the encouragement of innovation. Solesbury (1982) lists a wide range of government incentives for the development and application of new techniques. These include MAP (Micro-electronics Applications Project) and MISP (Micro-electronics Industry Support Programme) both of which have the objective of increasing industry's awareness of the application and development of products and processes embracing these new technologies. Other forms of support include Software Product Schemes (encouraging the development of software products), Technology Advisory Point (dissemination of British research expertise to commerce and industry), Computer Aided Design Centres (advising on the use of advanced computer techniques, as well as designing computer programs for individual firms), Robotics (supporting the manufacture and use of industrial robots) and a Support for Innovation Scheme, which is a general programme to provide help for research and development. Solesbury states that there are also several other specific schemes for flexible manufacturing systems, biochemistry, fibre optics and information technology.

All this adds up to a totally uncoordinated picture, a locational scramble, a funding gamble. The market, given its head, will respond but the market is notoriously inefficient and high-tech resources are too valuable to be wasted in a *laissez-faire* nightmare. If this is presenting a firm argument in favour of strong regional planning then so be it. Some 'regions' already have clear advantages; the Thames Valley has universities, the M4, Heathrow, an attractive environment, high-quality housing, an already established high-tech industry investment. Yet further investment in it needs the support, direction and security of a regional plan as equally as those areas with little present attraction. Cheshire and West Central Scotland are other 'regions' which would benefit from regional planning. It is only through such forms of control and direction that the grave disadvantages of market saturation can be avoided, and the true future potential of high technology in Britain can be best realized.

Nonetheless it would be dangerous to attempt to forecast accurately the future spatial form of high-technology developments. An era of explosive new dimensions is in the offing. Brzezinski has pointed us to it but in Valéry's (1962) words 'if historical experience is anything to go by, the outcome will betray all expectations and falsify all predictions'.

References

Hall, P. and Markusen, A (1982) *Innovation and Regional Growth: A Proposal for Research*. Institute of Urban and Regional Development, University of California, Berkeley (unpublished).

Saxon, R. G. (1982) Designing for high technology. *Architects Journal*, 21 April.

Segal, N. (1982) *Science Parks – a British and American Overview*. Conference paper presented at TCPA, London, 11 November.

Solesbury, W. (1982) *National Policy Issues*. Paper presented at CALUS Conference on Development for High Technology, London, 2 December.

Valéry, P. (1962) *Collected Works*. London.

Worthington, J. (1982) Industrial and science parks – accommodating knowledge based industries, in *Planning for Enterprise*. Proceedings of an international seminar, Swansea, September.

10

High technology
and regional-urban policy

PETER HALL and ANN R. MARKUSEN

*High-tech industry is neither the saviour of
old industrial areas, nor directly the creator
of employment for the displaced industrial worker.
What, then, should be the priorities of urban
and regional policies if we are to reap the
benefits of the new Industrial Revolution?*

The main conclusions of this book emerged early on, and have been
often repeated. The first concerns the geography of high-technology
firms, and takes the form of a paradox: though high-technology industry is not bound to certain locations by reason of scarce or bulky
materials, or ties to immediate markets, nevertheless it shows a
pronounced tendency to cluster in a few locations and to appear
hardly at all in many others. The second concerns the pronounced
tendency for these favoured sites to be detached from, or peripheral to,
the older urban seedbeds of innovation. The third concerns the
geography of high-technology employment, and again consists in a
paradox: high-technology industry does not directly generate nearly
so many jobs as is commonly supposed, but its major impact may be in
the form of jobs indirectly created through the demands of high-
technology employees. Putting these three together, we conclude that
failing some very positive state intervention, a relatively few favoured
places will generate a modest number of high-technology jobs and a
much larger number of service jobs dependent on them.

The evidence presented in this book makes a rather strong case that
both in the United States and in Britain, an ensemble of leading
innovations has been restructuring the pattern of regional growth.
The contemporary leading sectors, which emerged in the upswing of
the Fourth Kondratieff long wave after World War Two, are built
around innovations in aeronautics, electronics, communications and
scientific instruments. These innovations have been adopted by – and
in turn have fuelled the growth of – distinctly new corporate
organizations. They were not picked up by the older sectors associated

with previous long waves: steel, cars, chemicals and even electrical machinery. By and large, the entrepreneurs in the current lead sectors were newcomers to business. Universities and governmental research moneys do seem to have played a more important role for these sectors than they did in the previous wave of innovative industries that took off the late nineteenth century, as evidenced especially by electronics and biotechnology.

In the United States, it is quite clear that the new high-tech businesses are disproportionately found in locations outside the traditional American manufacturing belt. The commercialization of most of the products in these new sectors occurred after World War Two, some even more recently, and plants producing them have generally shunned the American industrial Heartland. One reason for this seems to be that the previously-developed industrial complexes actually played a repellent role. After World War Two, the Chicago-to-New York belt rapidly converted back from wartime production of airplanes, tanks and other *materiel* to cars, domestic appliances, agricultural machinery and other domestic goods to meet pent-up wartime consumer demands. On that basis, for the two following decades it continued to perform well; the products of the third Kondratieff wave were still in demand during the first half of the fourth, until the product-profit cycle made itself felt in a falling rate of growth in demand coupled with increasing import penetration from newer industrial nations. Further experimentation with aerospace was left to the Sunbelt, leaving the Heartland dominated by executives of older-established sectors like cars and steel, and in turn creating an Upas Tree effect in the economies of places like Detroit and Pittsburgh. The same went for Britain, where the new industries generally located in the less industrialized areas of southern England, largely avoiding the older industrial areas of the north.

But it was not simply the repulsion of the new ideas by the old centres that led to the Sunbelt's capture of the bulk of the new high-tech development (Glasmeier, Hall and Markusen, 1983). The role of government research and development laboratories, which are more highly dispersed than corporate R&D (Malecki, 1981), played an attractive role; so did the disproportionate effect of military spending, especially for bases and prime contracts, toward the south and west. Almost certainly, the same factors operated in the genesis of the M4 Corridor west of London, as Breheny *et al.* suggest in their chapter. High-tech sectors, free of the market and resource considerations which predominated in the location of older, heavy manufacturing, are by most accounts oriented towards locations with a highly-skilled labour force and the amenities to anchor them there.

Yet both these features can be built into the environment. Indeed, practically the entire Silicon Valley labour force has been recruited over thirty years from other locations, and the excellent schools and superior housing stock that keep them there have been constructed for that very purpose. The opportunity to profit from land development may have played no small role in the orientation of original high-tech firms to locations like Silicon Valley, Orange County, the Dallas suburbs, and similar areas. Further, the prominent role of defence contracting in the process of new high-tech building, particularly in early stages, meant that the cost-plus system permitted new firms to recruit and pay for the relocation of personnel from other regions (Markusen, 1984a). Proximity to military bases, as noted in Saxenian's chapter, may also have been an attractive force.

Whatever the initial circumstances that led to the siting of new high-tech complexes, their growth is undoubtedly attributable to the agglomerative forces in their evolution. Saxenian shows how commercial applications of military-sponsored electronics led to the agglomeration of semiconductor, computer and communications firms in Silicon Valley; Hall *et al.* show how software firms currently insist on having that same address. The aircraft – now aerospace – industry on the outskirts of Los Angeles drew around it a similar set of electronics and communications firms, to form the basis of the San Fernando Valley and Orange County success stories shortly after World War Two. Both user and supplier industries form portions of this new high-tech complex, as well as complementary products like software.

Two developments, in fact contradictory, will condition the future possibilities of dispersion from these special centres. On the one hand, as the profit cycle model predicts, the ability of modern firms to uncouple production from research and development activities will lead to the decentralization of simpler mass-production activities. This will be specially true for cases where the region of origin has little room for expansion, thus putting pressure on housing, transportation and land costs – as is now the case in Silicon Valley and may become true for the M4 Corridor. However, other regions within the national economy may not be the beneficiaries; already, semiconductor assembly has leapfrogged American domestic locations for export platforms in the Third World.

On the other hand, the automation of the more routine portions of the production process may bring manufacture back home to the United States or Great Britain. Electronic components are close to being assembled by numerically controlled machines and robots. These high-tech production processes may result in the redomestication of production – though without much impact on employment levels in the industry.

However, to the extent that the process of innovation is far from complete, these agglomerations may continue to flourish. Certainly this was true throughout the 1970s. California, the lead state in both computer and semiconductor employment in the 1970s, continued to capture the lion's share of American high-tech growth; indeed, it *increased* its national share of semiconductor jobs over the decade (Markusen, 1984). As long as product (as against process) innovation, in particular, continues to preoccupy high-technology entrepreneurs, this agglomerative process will continue – to the frustration of neighbouring and competitive locations. And the importance of military and space-related manufacturing to the high-tech sectors ensures that product innovation will continue, since the obsolescence of products like missiles, fighter planes, bombers, submarines, space capsules and guidance systems, as well as smaller parts, is ensured by the very nature of the arms race.

This, as we already noticed at the end of Chapter 1, spells trouble for the older industrial regions and cities: Central Scotland, North East England, South Wales, Wallonia, the Ruhrgebiet, St Louis, and the whole American manufacturing belt from Chicago to Boston and New York. For by and large, the new industries are growing where the old industries are not; declining industries, and the attitudes that go with them, appear positively repellent to the growth of new entrepreneurship. The new captains of industry are attracted to places untouched by the old traditions: places previously agrarian and small-town in character, with a good (if largely man-made) physical and social environment, and with good communications both internally and with the wider world. This is the quality both of Silicon Valley and the M4 Corridor.

The difference, favourable to the United States and possibly fatal to Britain, is that there are a whole host of American examples and only a very few British ones. For the great 3000-mile crescent, from the Carolinas through Florida and Texas to Arizona, California and the State of Washington, Britain could substitute only a narrow 100-mile corridor that runs fitfully from Southampton and Portsmouth, across the M4 Corridor, to Milton Keynes and Cambridge. And even within that belt, the real sources of innovation are spottily concentrated on only half-a-dozen or so places.

These places, perversely, are in general the very locations from which British government policy has been trying to steer new industrial growth over the thirty-year period since World War Two. The supreme irony is that while government policy was taking away with the one hand – that of traditional stick-and-carrot regional policy – it was giving with the other, that of science and education policy. There was a total and apparently unappreciated schizophrenia in the British government's regional and urban development policies.

Though America has had no specific regional policy like Britain's, it has had a set of urban policy initiatives – and the end-result has been strangely similar to the British experience. While America has a wider spread of high-technology centres, it too is marked by a series of high-tech complexes which are highly concentrated in specialized centres along the nation's southern and western rims – in places like Silicon Valley, Southern California, Denver-Boulder, Austin-San Antonio, Greater Dallas, central Florida and the Research Triangle of North Carolina. In this case, military base location, government research and development funding, and defence procurement practices appear to have constituted the real industrial-regional policy. Together, the impacts of these programmes actually counteracted the whole series of efforts – stretching from Johnson's Model Cities to Carter's National Urban Policy – that tried to shore up the troubled cities of the nation's manufacturing belt.

The likelihood is that left to itself, the immediate future will uncannily resemble the recent past. However the map of regional aid is redrawn, left to themselves the industries of the coming industrial revolution are most unlikely to locate in the old industrial cities, and most likely to cohere to major universities and research institutes attached to smaller towns of good environmental quality in the British and American sunbelts. At most, there is the prospect that – following the model of Boston's Highway 128 close to MIT, or Carnegie-Mellon in Pittsburgh – a select few older industrial cities will attract some of the new industry through the presence of major universities or research institutes. But there will not be many of these.

Two quite different arguments can be made about this, with very different resulting policy prescriptions. The one stresses the difficulty of shifting the locational preferences of the new industries, and concludes that the right policy would be to encourage their growth wherever they happen to be. The other stresses the resulting social costs to the older industrial regions, and concludes that there should be a new integration of regional-urban policy with educational-scientific policy with the specific aim of helping those regions acquire a new high-tech base. Though they appear to point in opposite directions, perhaps it is possible to integrate them to some degree.

The first argument – we can call it the argument for passivity in the face of the trends – is that the right policy may be to accept that new industries will grow in new locations. In Britain, interestingly, there is a set of official policies that do this. The South East Strategic Plan, in 1970, established a set of major growth centres around London at distances between 70 and 130 kilometres (40–70 miles). Three – South Hampshire, Reading–Wokingham–Aldershot–Basingstoke and Milton Keynes–Northampton – lie directly in the main high-technology axis of southern England. The plan's major features have been somewhat scaled down and watered down since 1970 – but they survive.

The problem is that in detail, they are deficient. They do not cover the city of Cambridge, because that is in the East Anglia region – and Cambridge, where new computer and biotechnology firms have been spawned from research in university laboratories, is an archetype of the growing places of Britain. At present, local planning policy there – reinforced by central government – is to place a 15-mile green belt around the city, extending almost to join the London green belt. This means that the development of an M11 corridor is being systematically inhibited by official policy, though it is tending to happen anyway willy-nilly. The answer would lie in the designation of a science city close to Cambridge, and preferably on the London side – perhaps through an expansion of Harlow new town in Essex, proposed and rejected in the early 1970s, perhaps through a major expansion of the overspill town of Haverhill just across the Suffolk border. Here, development of Stansted as third London airport could clearly play a catalytic role. But better internal communications would also be needed – above all by road between Cambridge, Milton Keynes and the M4 Corridor west of London.

So a reorientation of traditional regional planning policies would surely be needed (Regional Studies Association, 1983; Department of Trade and Industry, 1983). In this view of policy, Britain would need to re-learn what it has tended to forget: that economic development must come first, that the kind of economic development now expected will have its own locational needs and preferences, and that planning will ignore these at its – and the country's – peril. Planning, in Britain since World War Two, has too often become an economic straitjacket. British planners – so this argument runs – now need above all to show that growth can be reconciled with sensitive conservation and with imaginative and sympathetic new design. It is a real and daunting challenge to a new generation of planners.

The alternative argument is that economic development without regional planning is bound to prove excessively costly to countries which are hard-pressed in an increasingly international world market. Continual spatial reshuffling of production activities absorbs large portions of national resources, in both public and private sectors, to build new urban environments while older ones are rendered prematurely obsolete (Markusen, 1977). These resources might other-wise have gone into refurbishing the basic industrial plant, national urban and transportation infrastructures, and non-defence-oriented research and development. The national opportunity cost of pouring more concrete on America's deserts or southern England's green acres, and more generations of weapons technology on the scrap heap, may not be small.

The planning implications of these considerations are clear. Regional and urban policy cannot be formulated or practised separately from some of the other national policies which have played an active role in the spatial shaping of high-tech development activities. Education and science policy in Britain, and defence spending in the United States, are two such policy areas. An evaluation of the social and opportunity costs of such policies, especially in unanticipated urban and regional restructuring, should be incorporated into decision-making. There may be good reasons for the greenfield siting of new high-tech complexes; but the longer-term consequences, especially in the undermining of older industrial complexes, should be borne in mind. At the same time, selective development of high-technology industrial growth in older industrial regions should be encouraged, especially as 'anchor sectors' for the rejuvenation of their regions. Regional policy, now, must come to terms with the new realities before it is too late.

These two arguments may appear to point in diametrically opposite policy directions. But it is possible to reach agreement on some critical points. Even if much of the new high-tech industry will continue to grow in new areas, that does not mean abandoning all of the older industrial regions and cities to decay and eventual death. Some of them, possessing skills and entrepreneurial traditions peculiarly appropriate to the new high-technology industries, may experience industrial renaissance. The experience of Scotland's Silicon Glen, in the thirty-year period since the mid-1950s, shows this; so does the development of Highway 128 in the Greater Boston area; so, potentially, does the experience of Pittsburgh. These areas seem to have succeeded because they are blessed with a concentration of scarce human infrastructure in the form of prestigious universities with strong technological traditions. For every one of these places, there may be a dozen lacking the necessary base. But, even if only one could be identified in each major older industrial region – a relatively modest and practicable policy prospect – that would provide a pole for future high-tech development.

This would require a major upheaval in ingrained decision-making structures. Nothing is more evident, from the experience of the work in this book, than that regional-urban policies and educational-scientific policies have been developed in separate, almost water-tight compartments. This is true even in a country like Great Britain, where both have been concentrated at central government level; in the United States, where responsibility is divided between the Federal and State governments, the division is quite evident.

For the future, for this policy shift to occur, there would have to be a new integration. The development of major research universities would need to be fostered by research policy, and would require support in the form of government research establishments in selected older industrial centres. All this would need to be harnessed to the needs of a new national policy for the development of new technologies for peaceful purposes – as is being done, consciously and evidently with some success, in Japan. This book has described the location of the new technologies of the fourth Kondratieff long wave. The critical question now is what combination of policies will shape the location of the even newer technologies of the fifth Kondratieff just about to begin. And here, the possibilities are still quite open.

References

Chinitz, B. (1960) Contrasts in agglomeration: New York and Pittsburgh. *American Economic Review*, **51**, pp. 279–89.

Department of Trade and Industry (1983) *Regional Industrial Development* (Cmnd 9111). London: HMSO.

Glasmeier, A., Hall, P. and Markusen, A. R. (1983) Recent evidence of high-technology industries' spatial tendencies: a preliminary investigation. University of California, Berkeley, Institute of Urban and Regional Development, Working Paper No. 417.

Malecki, E. (1981) Government-funded R&D: some regional economic implications. *Professional Geographer*, **33**, pp. 72–82.

Markusen, A. (1977) Federal budget simplification: preventive programs v. palliatives for local governments with booming, stable and declining economies. *National Tax Journal*, **30**, pp. 249–58.

Markusen, A. (1984*a*) Defense spending and the geography of high tech industries. University of California, Berkeley, Institute of Urban and Regional Development, Working Paper No. 423.

Markusen, A. (1984*b*) *Profit Cycles, Oligopoly and Regional Development*. Cambridge, Mass: M.I.T. Press.

Regional Studies Association (1983) *Report of an Inquiry into Regional Problems in the United Kingdom*. Norwich: Geo Books.

Index